T0278276

cahier

Friederike Mayröcker

Translated by
Donna Stonecipher

LONDON NEW YORK CALCUTTA

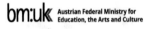

This publication was supported by a grant from the Austrian Federal
Ministry for Education, Arts and Culture, and the Goethe-Institut India.

Seagull Books, 2024

Originally published in German as *cahier* by Friederike Mayröcker

© Suhrkamp Verlag, Berlin, 2014
All rights reserved by and controlled through
Suhrkamp Verlag, Berlin

First published in English translation by Seagull Books, 2024
English translation © Donna Stonecipher, 2024

ISBN   978 1 8030 9 326 0

British Library Cataloguing-in-Publication Data

A catalogue record for this book is available from
the British Library

Typeset by Seagull Books, Calcutta, India
Printed and bound by WordsWorth India, New Delhi, India

cahier

"for a second for an eyeblink her face was soft and sorrowful, maybe (she) was lighting up a morrow &c. some terminology of fishes, sat like a bundle on the (toilet) = little toile and fondled the gardens .... <u>like regardez</u>, it was raining heavily like LOERKE, golden-yellow asters stuck to my cheeks (on the stone floor, say you), like fur, like the nice thick fur of the upper forests, you stood at the summit of the upper forest as the asters with their denticles on the stone floor as the tears down your cheeks .... it was 7 it was in the morning it was the aster's little head, how it trembled : my raining heart &c., half lying, half sitting on my bed : powerful genes. The singular emotion during penetration, you say, I remember, after opening my eyes, having written on the envelope the address of Eleonore F : written MARCH : thinking of Marchfeld (because it separated 2 cities lying across from each other) with mincing steps along the fields along the edge of the fields : <u>fairy-spook</u>, JD, as in the MARCH where Eleonore F lived, you say, the boundary of the soul, n'est-ce pas .... as for those pelisses : those hoods, you say, I observe that ever-oftener YOUNG PASSERSBY (flitting past me) hide under : in them or also OVER-OVERALLS, you say, I notice that YOUNG PASSERSBY (on bicycles) as I walk through the streets of the city "<u>the rest of Rembrandt, for example</u>," are wearing these pelisses or hoods, JD, <u>to flush me out</u>, and I discovered the pressed : compressed : dead insect between the pages of the book. I shoveled it in, <u>1 gesture of gloire</u> : namely, the roses of the Philharmonie and suchlike, I mean, I remember how hard it was for me already back then = 2005 = in the Hotel Sandlord, to walk up the hemp-mat-covered staircase to the 3rd floor, that is, my legs

"quit on me" as they say : <u>eternally</u> calls the memory to me &c.
ach to cut

                                                                    my
breath short we slipped, namely, into that café near the Lerchenfeld
Church since it was raining, raining pincushion flowers, and they
were shedding their needles before my very eyes, cheeks, and chin"

19.12.12

GEWIDMET:

beim
Kiesertraining :
meinersüßen: boxenden
mickeymouse

!

DEDICATED TO:

while doing
Kieser training :
my sweet : boxing
mickeymouse!

("Adam Elsheimer's *Flight into Egypt*") measures only 31 x 42 cm ....

Maria had drawn nigh, encounter with all kinds of animals and trees
: drowned moon, I mean, I saw the moon perish in the pond, I saw
the wingèd moon plunge, into the pond. They <u>licked</u> Him : ox and
mule : since He was swaddled in bandages = <u>adornment of the
bushes</u> and salamanders .... "pray.read.flee.keep silent.rest." =
from an old directive for monks found in Angelo Giuseppe Ron-
calli, blessèd art thou my beloved : my finger on your mouth.
Joseph stroking Him with a bird feather .... (well I mean, at our
age it's all only symbolic) : what varies is what is constant, isn't it
so. Joseph marching through flowers that with wide-open eyes :
Joseph standing in flowers that with bird feather and grass blade,
mule and Milky Way weeping willow and beech branch Joseph's
flambeau .... <u>in the name of God</u>, ach <u>the Institute of Sm.
Vipers</u>, of course the fine white birch trunks, the Big Dipper and
Cassiopeia, the falling Evening Star .... shall we bibliomance?
now I'm careful not to cut myself on the reed leaf on the floorlet
i.e. droplet of blood = pink petals columbine, I say, what profession
on the Sabbath, etc.

> ("in my finale, I say, I was self-conscious, well I mean, I
> think it was on a different day, maybe before noon or early
> in the morning, that I composed 1 few lines. It feels like it
> was a long time ago, unfortunately I am presently unable
> to meet anyone, I am psychically unwell and cannot bear it,
> thank you for your understanding, but I can't help it, &c.")

25.12.12

"beautiful mountains you know Via Harmonie in the window maybe beautiful mountains but actually beautiful clouds do you know that the tears. The crinkled bougainvillea from the island, upper forest &c. the crinkled bougainvillea on the desk I mean colored like the dawn ("perhaps he DISTRACTS himself 1 little, n'est-ce pas ....") that it deduces, my heart, this blissful wound SPELLBOUND on a mountainside 1 drop of dew you know ach my indolence .... how it sparkles, your eye, in this film "Tabu" I saw a pelican sitting motionless on a branch looking at me, then a pale cricket folded out of paper. Also, 1 x after his death 1 cricket landed on the windowsill, then it flew inside and settled onto the bookcase and there it stayed a long time until one day it died, in the end it seemed to grow stiff, you know, like a mummy, I didn't dare touch it, presumably Institute of Sm. Vipers"

"since I stuff pieces of cake into myself these days, and bamboo branches, namely it was cropped, the day's tail = the night (little dog with cropped tail galloping past the Roman sun &c.), I remembered a bouquet of white roses in a jar (le kitsch), 1 birdlet between the pages of a book : when I opened it the little bird fluttered up, a flowery scent when I opened the window in June, mats of spruce needles on a forest path in R., the assonance of his toe- and finger-nails, dead little dog galloping rose bushes in the shadow of the elms as if I were carrying finches into the wind, everything would have been nicer had you been there, you say, ach, you stuffed the dumplings. His foot which, crooked with noble firs ach this feverish butterfly, you say, star sparklings in the little fire-garden little gold chains on the Christmas tree &c., around 6 : snow-sky, metal tower, crane: like a Hopper, you say, what colors, you say, end of December, violet KAIROS, I am dazed, 'twas 1 other day that I (composed) these lines &c. Back then when Father was doing his

military service in Störmede, every day he wrote us a letter : con-
templative letters on the leaflets of the trees on the gray undersides
of the leaflets of the trees and how they rotated in the wind, I cried
over them .... in a subterranean room where I hide and feel safe
among these cushions, I hide and close my eyes and fall into a deep
sleep &c., actually I'm anxious before my nightly entrance into the
oubliette &c. and thus keep waking up, walking around in my
room, I espy the nocturnal birds in the violet sky through the win-
dow and follow, I mean, this ornament of the meadow 29.12
then while sitting, I felt dizzy .... "

29.12.12

"I don't need anything else anymore, don't need anyone else any-more. Just this one irreplaceable person whose hand. I mean whose hand explains the world to me, I mean as soon as I (feel around) for this person's hand ...."

1.1.13

"ach if I kindled a fieldfare namely at El Greco's feet so a blazing beauty <u>all your sm. shoulders</u>, I thought you were an evening-beauty, said Michael H., such rosy-throated wishes .... before us, the galloping future. The feverish butterfly <u>I was still small</u> burgeoning in the little fire-garden my foot 1 bit crooked with noble firs, &c. <u>This little bell</u>, you say, that from one of your nostrils .... you had powdered = <u>curled</u> the little lock of hair over your eyes, hadn't you. One has a kind of VISION as a writer : like Via Harmonie for instance : had this BRANCHLET VISION for years, the houseplants charged at the sun, 2 flaming candles = ornament of the meadow, this was the ecstasy and as I awoke at 4 o'clock in the morning it blew into my room and I saw everything <u>blurred</u> and I cried because a great anxiety had seized hold of me and I was frightened for my eyesight .... Waltzes after the glittering mountains like Wollschläger's "Herzgewächse." You're 1 dreamer aren't you. I'm a little ashamed, but I got carried away by my feelings, Francis Bacon with wide-open mouth devouring himself, "You were taken from me?," "I hungered after Jean" (JD) : I hungered after you, 3 days and nights <u>scattered / writing on scraps</u> then I couldn't go on I was suffocating I was shadowed most by mourning / by sorrow, you say, all the way to the end-cadenza, you say, our last secrets, you say, we hide even from our dearest friends / our dearest beloveds, someone from our circle of friends tended to employ 1 certain ADAGE which I am hereby adopting. I hereby adopt it and am proud that, from now on, I shall employ it as my own .... but we wanted to buy some incense, didn't we, in a hippie shop : you and I, and my room which I always fumigated after the release of the Holy Ghost etc., and one of us would dip our fingers into the holy water and FLICK them in the 16 cardinal directions .... but you always, I say, sutured my little arms, back then when the astronaut set foot on the moon we were sitting in the rosebushes with our arms around each other, it was the hour in which the astronaut mounted the moon and we were sitting in the bushes of the institution making love (you always sutured my little arms &c.) 1 x it happened to me at dawn, on the packaging, braille, Rax, Schneeberg (snow-mountain) shivering in her snow &c., we spent the morning in Café Hummel, words like clouds in parentheses = Oswald Egger. Pincushion flowers, as for the host of them on this meadow, in a subterranean room or when I was attacked, I mean when someone lifted a hand against me on my way home at night, e.g., I could not defend myself I could only <u>hurl</u> myself flat upon the earth

flat upon the earth what rapture, I STIPPLED. In a trice, I say, I cried nights, "<u>Dust Breeding</u>" on Marcel Duchamp, coocooing little bird back then, pinions of the mountains .... it lasted approximately 1 hour, you know, my seeing everything BLURRED"

5.1.13

"anthem anthem, I was shadowed by sorrow, we snuggled in Berlin and, namely, sighed after each other. Ribbon to mark one's place in the new calendar : lady-of-the-snows flowers in the mountain range like the cog railroad at the summit of the Schneeberg, I mean on the kitchen floor the dried (grieving) rose petal, yolk-colored with a pink edge almost like a small apple, shaped like a shell .... "when the sun flaunteth" the Lord lets it be sung in the branches, listened to THE KINKS : this Jupiter jubilation in the GRAMO. In a trice, I say, pinions of the mountains, cried nights

"write down what you saw : what is and what will occur afterward : the heavens retreat'd like 1 scroll that was rolled up, &c."

"that explains the world to me, the hand that I grasp ...."

you're 1 dreamer, aren't you, lianas rushes or lances : singing forth out of a fractured fish body, sm. plastic tub with teats. This was the ecstasy : the winter is so eternal almost 1 year &c., and musing as clouds drift. As back then the skylark ("all here") or the rest of Rembrandt (JD), ach write me what you see in a book &c., he planted kisses on my coat actually they were kisses on my body : I can hear his voice blooming, like anemones. Our winter quarters as we entered Café Sperl and Valérie B. whirred up to us, silvery .... ach Haydn's, I was still small, today a long walk with MAMA, "everything would have been nicer," says MAMA, "had you been there" .... I mean back then when we were living on Sarrazinstrasse in Berlin, Marianne's white shirt hung over the wicker basket, you know, and as for the scrubby gardens in front of the buildings (= patrols) the honey moon floated over Berlin. Lady-of-the-snows over Berlin, Marianne's white shirt over the wicker basket in the morning as if she had left this star. Goldfinch at my feet, a tear wells up, bluetit's wing like an ice crystal, ingrown, with addicted eye .... ach robin redbreast, ach heart-on-sleeve. Ach my faded remembrances, and tiptoeing to the sheet of paper already in the typewriter as to a beloved in the early morning in order to keep dreaming (my FADED remembrances) ach Grandmother stroking me : I was still small : she laid her hand on the back of my hand and I said, how warm your hand is .... namely the fairy-spook &c. As for this pincushion flower, I say, Mother's favorite flower, ornament of the meadow wasn't it (I can't keep anything to myself I blurt everything out. Rosebushes galloping past the Roman sun &c.), the Hofmanns, you know, while the younger violet = daughterlet, in the photo, with silk ribbons in her hair : fevered early spring in the photo : curriculum of language, you know .... (crêpe de Chine, loved him unto madness &c.)"

7.1.13

"that objects (slip) from my hands as if the ground itself were attracting them .... of course the color green, flattered the eye, I say, at the Vienna River the shrieking seagulls <u>flying flags</u> like that time at the pier in Trieste : unforgotten that early morning the lighthouse on the far shore in the east, unforgettable, you know, Trieste, 2 days, alone, the sea washing around my bare feet, almost nighttime that time, unforgettable Trieste (triste? no! high spirits you know (in which lifetime was that?), Trieste, the <u>steep</u> candelabra I clasped so that the sea wouldn't float—drag—<u>bawl</u> me out : I was alone I was still young what was I thinking, that time in Trieste, I mean the sea, the tall streetlamps on the beach, and how the waves, my bare feet. Mornings against a hemorrhaging horizon the revolving light of the lighthouse .... how long did I stand there on the beach, or did I cower half the night?)

"DOE HARE" as Elke Erb wrote in a poem, always this fate over one's head, <u>my darling lamb</u>, my fading world, I cried from sunup to sundown &c., this incomparable place where I trembl'd, that with the eyes <u>the dumb broad</u> the jagged hair .... per Samuel Rachl, Sacred Heart on the display

would leave me behind, panting, namely, loving you unto madness. Went into Café DOMMAYER, after the heart-checkup I mean the shadow-checkup, you know. And you could remember the events, so that we both had the same memories—if I ask you, e.g., do you remember back then in the DOMMAYER many years ago we sat outside under the <u>lisping</u> leaflets I mean woodlets, and you immediately call out, yes, I remember, back then in the DOMMAYER

under the lisping leaflets through which the blue of the sky <u>seeped</u>
&c.

   so, the shoreline = Trieste lulled, lulled, with incense, I say.

<u>All stuffed animals,</u>

                      as in heaven,

                                .... "

9.1.13

green leaflets jammed in the drawer it made me cry so much the Barbara branch BURST into white blossoms : it brings blessings, my love, kiss me .... ach the little rivulet whirred. The eyne of the flowers, the source the sea the gecko the deep grotto .... "languishing on the most isolated mountains, ... to go over and to return, Hölderlin"

"the one who loves more is the needy one : he stands with outstretched hand and waits for a love-offering = feathered leaf nestles into apricot's cheek. Well I mean, the ferocious proliferation of gazes, I mean the garlands of her voice in the airs of Schiller Park, you know, divulging secrets (in the rose-net) as the chestnut trees began to bloom (Ulla namely) proclaiming the news, and us, shrieking across the grass, from sheer happiness, &c. Ach, they fanned out, the thoughts, do you remember, the memories, because the snowflakes of May, the wisdom of the anemones, the wreaths of spring your gleaming eye, ach .... well I mean : 1 black thread on the kitchen floor looped into a treble clef, till deep into the night so that I had to start crying : he recounted anecdotes, had always recounted the same anecdotes till so deep into the night that I had to start crying, you see .... this little brook how it flooded, driving leaves and wind before it, apples in the foliage ach clematis in the garden, and mostly I was flooded with sadness, "then from sheer emotion I just could not go on" &c., the Wellingtons printed with roses stood in the stairwell, you know, ach the twosome of cloud and meadow, how sm. girls SMELL, how have I become expired?, wandering around, let's be faithful to each other. Is there something in me—what is it? if only I could express what I feel, the paintbrush nearly slipped out of my hand. Did I dream (about) you? the light

that evening was so transparent it was like 1 moonlight $=$ <u>1 madness</u>
: you were wearing moss-colored stockings and shoes, at the edge
of the woods : all the more do the musical scores glow, I say, hope
that my eyes DUMB BROAD jagged hair .... diamantine namely
sweetbush, leaflet already SUPER September under Türkenschanz
hill, trading our shoes, stockings, caps, whispering secret codes, in
the trampled-upon grass &c., this flickering of the eyelids ("I was
still small, at the skating rink, winters, practicing the inside curve :
Mother, for hours. Freezing, watched me")."

12.1.13

\

"I mean garlands / I just let it fall, the object, I mean it slips from my hand as if the epicenter of the earth had attracted it to itself: jasmine of the earth marrow of the earth I mean as a *PILGRIM* as thoughts of flight or thoughts of snow, back then as the chestnut trees began to bloom (Schiller Park / The Horae) back then, and us, shrieking with happiness across the grass and fanning out, you know, as he BEDDED his hand on the back of my hand I mean floating, and his hand fanned out over my hand, and I called out "how soft, your hand" .... namely languishing into the heavens while the moon gaped : in the hurry of the wind (shattered, &c.) agitated, my soul, that is, enveloped in a sorrow, I mean the inconsolable day &c., mirror of the heart's Aurora : frantic, I thought I was losing my mind (hubris of age), the falling stars plummet into my boughs, you know, ach the sparrow in my lap is like 1 miracle, I say, in a trice &c., crippled as I am, I flew a flag at the dark-blue (sea) .... I have sm. siblings I have islands of order, little red poppy-soul and I always have to cry when you. Hubris of age, I'm cuckoo, amid the lilac bush's veiled branchlets, ach and dissolutely (I) went down the path, I'm drowning in tears (the pink tips of the mountains / mignonettes / madness protects just like fever, Chris Marker, bedded-down grass, after I'm already suffocating from having no one to talk to, you know, do you remember what a luxury of leisure we had in the fields and the stillness ....), back then when I asked him, "What about after death?" he said, "As in the time before I was born," namely in the subterranean room. And in the most extreme case : ZILCH, &c., with bird feather and grass blade, flowers with wide-open eyes .... Lady-of-the-snows in B., taking the lamb to heart. I need a contemplative life / I wear RABBIT FUR on my skin, ach the star in the eye of the nightingale &c."

15.1.13

"I saw that the morning stood in flames namely in its trinkets = in its teats, I saw the firelight in her armpit, saw the cherries and sun-fires in her eyes. Just let me go to seed, you know, I saw the yg. father : weeping in lilac Ajax, wasn't he, or woodlet .... it is a lot to write "blessed child" = to practice, but then endless amounts of MAQUILLAGE and flowers of the air. No this is not a diary it's a desk-puppet = death-presentiment, or as in those days : I was still small, my parents and I sitting on the Cobenzl hill with the patient BELIEVER who gave me 1 little dancing doll, that summer night, in flowercolors, whereas the wafting cloths in my left eye, 17.1. I am now in my Cubist phase, you see, resting in God's lap : 1 lark-song namely, I wrote and wrote as though I wanted to give up the ghost : this morning 1 slipping sledding : this morning entering into 1 consciousness-void, that must be what dying is like, which is to say I hung on his lips while he ran riot in my little heart, and I, leaving this world's lovely moil .... DIRECT garden-glory, you know, chic of the sm. Minervas. Anecdotally e.g. that the necklace hung in the branches of the Christmas tree &c., howling (even) and beyond the wild ass the wafting breast &c. As if I wanted to lose my mind, I say, the green bandion of your soul, I say, ach actually it's the bushes that are declaiming .... Bernadette H. told me how her mother had died : on that evening a fierce storm was raging, and "she just up and went off with the storm" .... Bella! he said, as we parted. All phenomena lulled, the shoreline of Trieste (I blew on your cold fingers because my mouth gave off both warm and cool air, didn't it, I also CHEWED on your fingers, munched your hand &c., dew-bedecked = the shoulders of the butterfly, iridescent and strange the dyed eyebrows of the landscape I mean we wanted to go to a café, or move from one café to another : with gimmicks. To the Drechsler, to the Sperl, to Café Museum, to the Dommayer, 'twas infatuation, &c.) Dearest friend, <u>lickety-split</u> : you know already : it's all about the body, at bottom it's all about the body : everything so DOWNSTAIRS, SWALLOW-TAIL : 1 crouching like a dog, you know, in the station concourse, such blossoms of RHINESTONE, which was 1 romanticizing (1 excrement in the bowl as I entered the bathroom : in the flophouse of Bohumila G., etched itself into my brain) .... In your head you take many journeys, he said, but when it comes to realizing them, you get cold feet, &c., "unto madness do I love you," I say, this incomparable unspeakable place, I say, the SPARROWS hopping, unshod, roses will-o'-the-wisp and rosemary, the gently lilting waves. And the wilting. Of the little lilac tree : puffing from summer, wasn't it ...."

18.1.13

"am so listless, but inexhaustible flow from the little beach scene (Trieste), helpless SANTÉ & equiv. Tiny Christmas tree, so tiny one could hardly see the IDOL (with ringlets grafted on its branches, nothing but chimeras, you say, and break off 1 bud, wintry reaching my hand through the park lattice I think it was Perchtoldsdorf &c.), fooled me, or his bare foot whispering from the little garden, lines : the wildest in the notebook, I have to cry so much because it's all so beautiful, in sleep's pilgrimage .... Tápies dead, he. I strolled through the meadow which was 1 bit slanted, with stars : soft blossoms namely étoiles. Forgot to tell you that my writings only ever had the idol of the "branchlet" in mind, feverishly distracted thoughts, midst the sea, of flowers, I say, detail of a painting by Fra Angelico, ach we sank into the cabbage white butterflies : poignant pensée, consumed me : ach insatiable bliss of the stars sparkling in the heavens .... but within my grasp, the mountains within my grasp; when the mountains are within my grasp on the tear-horizon, you say, 1 rain will fall, verses of a snow &c., which is why he dunketh his head in the airs which like shadowy ghosts, you say, ach, I had such a beautiful dream of a burning cliff-face (Heine), of flowers and friends, oh of a dry eye. I didn't know, had I really heard that gorgeous singing = jubilant boy's voice, or was it 1 dream, "I see clearly and I hear clearly and still, I'd rather be drunk," Hashimoto Kansetsu, I mean that thing with the <u>corncockles</u>, how they were poured out all over the meadow when I woke up and startled. And it was so early in the morning, and the storms : no, they didn't WHISTLE, it wasn't that they were whistling around the house, it was much more that they rumbled : bellowed : rampaged in the atrium namely. In the folds of the yellow duvet, the silhouette of a falcon or fawn was forming namely of such monstrous dimensions that I grew frightened = clouds in the distance : may you be protected. <u>My eyes are closing</u>

.... so I remember less the event itself than the SENTIMENT that enveloped the event, I say, milky such a heavenly morning = CLOUD PURÉE. The nights not to be borne : <u>nights of the rat</u>"

20.1.13

"ach the pilgrimage of sleep, n'est-ce pas, back then in Donaueschingen as we were admiring the rill, namely the source of the Danube, I mean we let the water trill over our hands : a baptism? you said, a sacrament? &c. .... but I can't take care of a husky, I say, if I can't even take care of a flower, I say, yesterday the bus 13A nearly ran me over, I say, wild and Kotzebue : name of a white wine, a butterfly. Kindled with my morrow. When you wrote *brütt*, said Ulla-Mae, you were *on top*; and with each subsequent book that you've written you have managed to reach that peak again, BUT NOT TO GO BEYOND IT .... every morning I opened up my coloring book and started coloring = smoking a lot, I need a contemplative life : no excitement, no change, took the lamb to heart (goldeye torn with veil), "the star in the eye of the nightingale," ach in the deepest winter of the woods, enveloped, I say, red petals of the autumn Adonis, the start of a saintly budding .... well I mean, it was last May when I thought, "now no more snow will fall," I mean it was definitive, the birds .... I mean but it was still cold &c., how do you manage, I ask the finches and chickadees, to survive the winter .... ach greetings from your life-cloud = rivulet from the mountains, I write to Anne Bennent, where to begin? When I saw you in the waiting room at my doctor's. At AM HOF, 1 text from many years ago spoken by you, the wind carried many of the words away so that I couldn't follow my own writing, and it was so icy-cold yesterday evening and I paced up and down and felt myself taken back to a cold early morning at the sea in Trieste. Talking is clearly a distraction from the essence = from writing, isn't it. Ely just after the holiday (Descent from the Cross) I sit in the train-station restaurant order a coffee and read ROLAND BARTHES BY ROLAND BARTHES. It takes about 50, 60 years to come to know oneself : to come up with a self :

namely "Little Imagination" also bitch is like kitsch, songs e.g. I would have grasped, before a dark-green grove &c. (24.1) I'm already looking forward to days spent together and <u>droning moonlight</u>, do we want these whitish bushes in the window : virgin's bower or snow (the over-excited artist)

       oh, withering time. Lily-of-the-valley bouquets, or, where shepherdesses"

24.1.13

"once, sitting next to me, he said, someday when I'm old, I'd like
to write poems : fragile fleet-footed figments, aren't they"

for Peter Handke
27.1.13

"called out, how soft your hand &c., I mean <u>fawned</u> into the heavens while the moon floated up, namely, in the flurry of winter my mind (went to pieces) &c., namely my mind, I say, must <u>give way</u> when I write. When it won't do that or can't, everything's a lie : and I am punished with illness or blind futility .... so flags, you know, before my eyes, white flags. I resisted learning to sew, JD, with much winding. When we can't see each other for even one day, I grieve and drown in tears, milky such heavenly events, ach I am so wretched that an INRI flushed me out of the deepest sleep &c."

for Edith S.
27.1.13

"is it OK, she asks, that I love my daughter like a lover, she says, that I love her as though she were my beloved : all day long I look forward to seeing her again. And then she <u>sets her sights on</u> 1 face unknown to me and WALKS RIGHT PAST me, and I burst into tears, namely"

for Elisabeth von Samsonow
27.1.13

"Papa trembles, or, dog becomes armchair : armchair dog, there's always one who loves more than the other, you say (30.1), over the Iron Hand to the maple trees and finally down into the valley where the sm. inn where I consumed my dinner. I was composing all night long, ach this quivering green in the window as I, flitting past, in the morning, some panicle, leaflet, or *butterflies* ("that's something I'd rather not tell you," he said, branchlets which, whirling, were the same shade as your eyes) .... in the sm. restaurant on Seegasse, where you kissed me while the softest rain. Your most recent letter of 6 November, with the red light in the background, presumably a red sunset, I mean this feeling of the snow-landscape &c. Eleonore F. sent me a haiku : "The bell fades away—the scent of blossoms wells up—that is the evening" (Basho), so I understand that that which lights up so is the SOUL, I find myself now in my Cubist phase, I shoveled into myself the roses of the Philharmonie &c. Ach how great was my anticipation = impatience : he would come at night (after the event), I could hardly stand it, I was wearing my lilac dress, and then it was almost midnight and I threw myself on the bed, crying : finally the bell rang and there he was at the door, and I was magnetized .... you darling lamb you forsaken world, "*winter my lovely*" .... unto madness do I love you, you say, this unspeakable place : roses, will-o'-the-wisp and rosemary, the gently lilting waves and the WILTING, of the feather-woodlet, puffing from summer ❤ Sacred Heart on the display do you remember under the leaf canopy of lisping branchlets in the garden of the DOMMAYER : through which the blue of the heavens seeped &c.)

.... craw of the toilet = little toile, I surrender to ruin. 1 argent in the trees, and in the corner of the living room, my time, like a fire, is dying down"

30.1.13

"I bump into objects that then fall over .... I would be lacking nothing ach the sparkling sky, back then I was in Graz with a sm. circle of friends, that is, the BOMBER TROUSERS, I say, and I was in love with .... but he went out of his way to avoid me : I grew thin, and when I passed by mannequins in shop windows I seemed to myself to be in a forget-me-not fever : branchlets that whirling took on the color of his eyes, 1 pastel-hued sky WHIRLED THROUGH by solitary winter birds &c., so that tears. Just now when I wanted to write down the next thought, it raced off—was it not as though my short-term memory in that second blinked, whereas the little fire-woodlet .... whereas he, I mean, INCITED the pale-blue rosettes of the little fire-woodlet = ("le kitsch" &c.), somehow I remember that it was getting dark on the Cobenzl or dark-blue thundering in early spring. Jesus Maria called out Luvík Kavín when I CABLED him that I couldn't come because I was sick, &c., ach, I sparkled in forget-me-nots as we, in Vienna Central Cemetery : I burst into tears because I was so old : and would soon end up there myself, between forget-me-nots and anemones, well I mean, when I buried him 13 years ago I let myself fall into his grave with a little bouquet of forget-me-nots in my hand, I mean somehow I can no longer sit in that restaurant "The Princesses" (because shivering from cold) .... at the gynecological exam he said, I'll do it with just my little finger, and then he showed me his little finger. That was 1 passion, I say, to (wipe) one's b. with one's fingers, it was 1 passion to see Mt. Blanc rise on the horizon every morning, with gimmicks, I say, the roaring of the landscape, winter '71 he wrote me, "I scared up 1 great place for us in Zehlendorf, there's even a nice dog : you'll be happy here" .... you see, it was last May when I thought (in my fire cabinet) now no more snow will fall, no birdlet I mean but it was still cold, &c.,

the sensations, you know, I say, for which one finds no words, as once Mother said before she left, "these sensations for which I find no words; the more sensations, the fewer words," actually she said that before she died, &c., these waterscapes, you know, ach these rivulets before her death in her eyes (that had lost their flowercolor back then, before her death). These worldviews, you say. What one can be for another, you say, one can be for another the kingdom of heaven, can't one, without the other, who is the kingdom of heaven for the first, knowing it. I mean sighing into the heavens while the moon floated namely in the flurry of the wind it (went to pieces) my mind, &c."

31.1.13

"1 gesture of splendor, today 2.2 = Candlemas (redeem us, oh Lord), today the candles on the Christmas tree should be lit for the last time, you say, namely, the mercy of the body. Everything is so transparent, recognizable, you say, and from a shadow emerge words and sentences, for example, the eyes tear up in the woods, we call out our names, we call out to each other because we have lost our way. The interior of your hand, the crow cleaves through the air, you say, like 1 dream over the rooftops 1 black rack of clouds .... all of it platitudes, little boxes of blueberries covered in hoarfrost silk, you say, branchlet, you say, woodlet lisping with incense, I mean in May I said to myself, now no more snow will fall, ach, the birdlets. That's how we snowed through this whole winter, you say, we checked off the days (as once Mother, before the day had even begun to decline), even though they could have been our last, that would have caused us 1 sorrow, already the flame of February was heralding itself. Do you remember : climbing the stairs to the alcoves high up in the Rüdigerhof, all afternoon, all night long, my beloved : ach your little swallowtail, your blonde hair .... in the corner of the living room, 1 argent in the trees, time is dying down on us. This unspeakable place, you say, back then in the south of France he said, if we're lucky with the weather, tomorrow we'll see Mt. Blanc rise into the sky, at the distance of the villa, namely, without having chewed it, I swallowed the piece of cake whole. "You are my daily bread," I say to him. "Is that clock repair shop still on the corner," I say to him, "so much has changed : I hardly go out anymore, &c." Hen with gloire or glory ach he fondled the garden .... how, the moon floated : sparkling of the heavens, but the winter's flurry (broke) my mind (into pieces), &c., addicted furs, the benevolence of the human soul etc., Morandi, the jugs. Sometimes like 1 cloth = 1 dove before my eyes .... how soft your hand I sighed into the heavens, namely in the sparkle of winter my mind went to pieces, th' rivulet from the mountains, lily-of-the-valley bouquets like shepherdesses .... that time we hiked to the source of the Danube, it originates in Donaueschingen, you say, I mean we let the fountainhead flow over our hands, and then, under the chestnut trees : that is, hallucinating (SHORTHAND) with intoxicated visages we moved under the chestnut trees, I mean it was early fall in the baptismal font of the Danube's flux we recited a Russian poet, unspeakable how the teardrop rolls down my face &c., "so give us innocent waters, oh pinions give us, to travel over and to return with truest minds" (Hölderlin)"

3.2.13

"the last dream-image in a succession of morning dreams : 1 man in a forest sitting on an embankment : his head framed by giant green coltsfoot leaves so that he can't look at the computer on his lap. It is not possible to tell whether he can type on the keyboard, whether he possesses arms at all. He seems to resemble a forest animal, I name him Felix while the proliferations of the forest QUIVER AROUND him like 1 litany, and so I cried after I had made a drawing of the dream-image : maybe it moved me because it put me in mind of Kafka's writings .... I spent CIRCA half an hour drawing this dream-image, and through it : namely through the salt of tears : the sensitive skin around my eyes started to crinkle. It crackled in the woodlet (in the Schweizergarten), I mean Heinz Schafroth would have enjoyed it, oh well. When one looked at Lake Biel = at the foot of the "*living room*," the waves of the lake glistered and glared so that I had to use my hand to shade my eyes : not so harmless, I mean the fervor of the sun wildernesses was SCALDING &c. ("Achi : the old guard") = I shaded these thoughts with my hand. Ach tear-stained kolkhozes = clothes, the blue morning, how beautiful the collages of the clouds, the crosshatching of the birds (5.2) .... I dreamed of water in a basin that threatened to spill over = the need to pass water, tuft of grass among a handful of dried blueberries, I say, where I fevered lightly where I saw the sagging

𝑓   on the bathing beaches I mean voluminous visage, how the teardrop rolls. Unspeakable sometimes, like 1 cloth before my eyes. Am so listless however, forever sobbing in riparian shrubbery, after the walk along the tree-lined road in Donaueschingen as we received the anesthesia and began to fever aloft verses into the autumn air .... while the SENTIMENT : mirroring of an event at the source of the Danube : rill that we let trill over our hands, I'm an *underdog*, you know, eternally sinking (the sm.

spoon) into applesauce &c. I mean gladiolas whose voices, in the
airs of Schiller Park, were revealing secrets.

> (Did you used to play POST OFFICE?
> <u>various</u>, dentures to take out, weren't
> there)"

5.2.13

der Wuchs des
Forstes

The proliferations of
the forest

"Thallo : feeling of blooming ach <u>heart-speech</u>, you say, ferocious proliferations of the forest 1 ultra sound. We often went to the GLORY where on Sundays and holidays 1 old violinist played, and we billed and cooed : 2 sm. swans on my table the steep flower-entwined stairway (e.g.), and while I drew myself up into greenery = copies of yg. swans .... I was in admiration of this poet : since I was reading this poet, also DOE HARE which stood in the corner of the bold tableau. Whereas this prose frequency made me suddenly <u>thirst</u> to write poems (ach, thistle bush : not in my hair!) Did you call out my name? so that I woke up, how beautiful the cross-hatching of the cloud delight, <u>when I was small</u> I sank down into a meadow. The phantasies of the night : did you call out my name in the early morning? I woke up because you (called &c.) out my name, &c. collages of clouds around your brow, you are my only consolation .... embroidered morning moon back then as we strolled through Wertheimstein Park, past the jasmine bushes, cap blown off by wind &c., certain permutation techniques in my writings, with a little grabber tool he lifted objects up off the floor, marched through lilies of the valley, embankment brambles, I would so like to go again to the "Little Café" (Franziskanerplatz), they treat me like 1 child &c., <u>when I was small</u> I sat in the handcart in D. and let myself be pulled by Mother. Father said, "The left eye is not reading along," they say she got into the bed he had vacated a few hours earlier, that way she could still be in his presence. We are racing toward Easter, I <u>wr.</u> a ginkgo, when one sees through the <u>various</u> vanities of one's friends, there is 1 friend e.g. who familiarized himself with our thoughts and habits .... now don't cry anymore, my love, on the GRAMO the piano suites of Handel, 1 gloomy day. Ach the little feather-forest's soul incited me, your eyes ("le kitsch") in the shade of pale-blue rosettes incited me,

to phantasize, while the little feather-forest's breath incited me,
<u>whirling</u>, to see the shade of the pale-blue rosettes of your flower-
eyes. Fading away, the eye, and wafting o clivia, namely the nimbus
: the Neckar River, the boughs in rain "balconette" agitated dreams
we frolic across the swept-clean Atlantic (fumbles the comma, the
em-dash) we're standing with our bicycles at the Atlantic amid a
wild resplendence of blue lupine &c."

8.2.13

"what sweet ears you have, amoretto, somehow, the songbirds showed up in flocks, like 1 FOG .... the pink Lilienthal teacup slipped out of my hand, fell to the floor : burst : <u>I was dumbstruck</u> I was just dumbstruck this word from past centuries stuck like a ringlet of hair on the duvet (the excrement was braided) I was <u>dumbstruck</u> when you began reading aloud, overnight the cut had healed up. <u>Bumping against</u> the bushes ruching and shrubs back then in R. as we sailed, through the airs, stumbling upward beflagged, you know, whipping out the camera in R., after we had gone through the underpass, SASHAYING namely, and then the hawthorn hedge, which pierced us : toppling into the hawthorn hedge, that time in R., while the blossoms of the hawthorn hedge <u>traced themselves</u> upon our bodies ....

> A snatch of sleep. Listen to me, I want to tell you what I dreamed : in a czar's palace I was honored with raspberries sweetened the drink he whom I loved did not love me back, Blueberry Hills this bitter cloud cloud of golden-blonde hair &c., the thing I had enjoyed marched straight through me, 12.2, deep snow, could walk again (in the dream), like a hunting dog racing off I buried myself in Bennington's portrait of JD .... how did you know that his illness broke out on his (tail), in the early morning the sleep I did not enjoy pressed down on my lids quivering green leafery, Baudelaires of longing ("le kitsch") sweetened with raspberries the drink &c.

Then the cook came and brought 1 second serving of mashed potatoes, he leaned in very close and said, "here, 1 supplement." Well I mean, to express it poetologically, in that book there were only cockeyed images it robbed me of my desire to keep reading namely that I saw myself so DEPICTED (like a shepherdess &c.). She let herself dream of something glittering, actually she had decided to let herself dream of something glittering ....

> and were you of such adornment : fleur and grass-bed, in the incunabulum of your sentiments, &c."

13.2.13

"I now have a garden in my kitchen a sm. Matisse in the linen closet
&c., you gave me a basket of grape hyacinths 1 little pot of spring
snowflakes : and were they of such adornment fleur and grass-bed,
your sm. shoulders I mean Haydn's hornbeams and *trophy* in the
allées, I mean, asylum and croco, ataxia of a nature which staggering
before my eyes, jagged little bird clothing drenched in tears the blue
morning, how beautiful the cross-hatching of the clouds, I would
so like to go again to the "Little Café" (Franziskanerplatz) ....
with a bang the dream was gone <u>I was dumbstruck</u> I had fallen
asleep in the dream I had woken up in the dream, where do you get
THE MEAT OF THE POEM, you asked me back then but I didn't
know, EvS enjoyed telling this anecdote : how we met <u>that time on
the train</u> (with the little dog Heinzi on her lap &c.) ....

> <u>drunk ach 1 rose</u>
> crescent moon WAXING I've
> gone to seed as though I
> were flying : 1 drop of blood, sm. Swiss pine :
> bed that Goethe died in

circa continuation of our dreams and tears from the previous night
ach leaning improbably at the open window, while standing we
entwined ourselves around each other : spring branches from
entwined trees, you say, and every year the same *performance*.
Everything so infinite phlox or fetish I <u>have gone to seed</u>, one
would need something pre-written = pre-thought, we were stand-
ing with our bicycles before the waves of the Atlantic when the call
from home came, <u>dear</u> cowering nude at the banister = Francis
Bacon .... landscape with cow = cow in front of wheatfield &c.
While blueness and fortissimo of feelings, you say, the Thaya made
speed, in the twilight &c. In my asylum or croco, I think it will
continue :

(<u>chirpeth</u>), my flatbread,

once a sm. bird lost its way in SWEETFLAG, well I mean, I had
(Man Ray's) "<u>Dust Breeding</u>" in my quarters"

15.2.13

"the braided excrements, namely, I began to fall into ruin : Les
Murray, the years gouge themselves into my face, on your hand
namely in icy camisole through the forest, branches on your blue
enclosure &c., the clouds like May blossoms in your lap, bloomed
(the spring snowflakes bloomed in the night, you know), now all
the world is one and the same to me. And we crashed into 1 genteel
bar so that we felt genteel ourselves, I mean wingèd : and those
BOUQUETS nearly smothered me as Marcel Beyer walked me
home = accompanied me like Jean Genet's garden of paradise ....
while the wide-open blossom-eyes of the hydrangeas (like Ann
Cotten's puzzle-blossoms of language). I borrow from my own
erstwhile texts, so, on the train as we CANOODLED : with the
little dog Heinzi on your lap &c., the clouds like May blossoms on
sumptuous trees in the ROSE GARDEN. We had fallen for each
other : whereas those yg. shoots from the chestnut tree (sawn-off
branches) lying on the lawn of the castle garden we wanted to take
1 few boughs home to (celebrate) that early spring, whereas jagged
birdlet .... we meet, for example, in Café Rüdigerhof, where some
deer. Those BOUQUETS nearly smothered me namely their scent,
Jesus Maria, said Luvík Kavín, I would not lack for anything if you.
Always in the evening = evenings, saying goodbye, in the morning
= early mornings locked in each other's arms, the sm. bird lost its
way in sweetflag = writing workshop, could not find its way to
freedom .... back then you said "you have eyes like an eagle's
etc." quivering greenery (longing) : "le kitsch" drink of a dream
sweetened with raspberries : 1 gesture of splendor. Ach sleep-
harmonics I am currently in my Cubist phase, then we hiked down
the Iron Hand and went into the sm. village inn .... he didn't say
anything he said only, "Madame, I hunger for your every line we
are calligraphing we are photographing your text," it used to

always <u>tear my heart out</u> but now it's all one and the same to me, you know, sometimes just 1 cloth in front of my eyes, unspeakable how my teardrop rolls, this (my) <u>vanishing without a trace</u> because no one listens to me, that is, sanding (sliding) in sleep : <u>in the church room</u>. And everything's cozy : wool blanket over my knees and working motif on my teacup "*bunch of forget-me-nots*" &c., I remember that on the Cobenzl it was getting dark or darkly thundering, it just depends on the transcendence, of the words, &c."

17.2.13

"am inconsolable, shall I not tell you the news, you say, when the turtle-doves chickadees and finches : <u>my sole desire</u> is to peer into the branches of the weeping willow and hop around with them and speak to them in my mother tongue : French. You love me you understand me when you let the Christmas tree, stripped of its ornaments and so merciful, stay in my little room, <u>it had once so kindled : flickered</u> &c. The mignonettes on your brow your countenance burned, on the photograph half-pines = recamiers .... bit of forbearance. At some point one cannot go on and just wants to sleep, while in the corner of the living room, time is dying down, do you remember, I say, our talk : "we walk for a long time in darkness, but then one day a bud breaks open and we behold the light" : circa platitude? these snow-roses in opaque white .... <u>I was dumbstruck</u> I was just dumbstruck, what sweet ears you have, the interior of your hand, l crow strides through the air, that's how we snowed through the whole winter, you say, so that you made it through the winter without falling, branchlet woodlet lisping from incense. All your sm. shoulders, in my asylum or CROCO I think it will go on : heart's chirping .... my flatbread, ever-longer rests on the recamier, I mean Linde Waber painted the flowers (under the snow-blanket) opaque-white, sweet spring snowdrops birdlet, you know (yellow budgies) "le kitsch" I surrender to ruin, in the corner of the living room, time is dying down on me, they almost smothered me the BOUQUETS as Marcel B. WALKED me home that night the blossom-eyes of the hydrangeas opened &c., I was <u>so wingèd</u>, as the deep night, descended, I thought <u>in my soul</u> in Venice (as the deep night, descended) .... the book of World Literature on the floor, Aunt H. at 90 still hot flashes"

(what is underway there, you know, the black sash. You were at my place but I was not at your place, you always asked me to come to your place but I came up with pre-texts for why I couldn't come .... you lay by my side without touching me : it was as if you wanted first to learn (me) <u>panicked</u>, that that which lights up so is the soul)

22.2.13

"sunk in 1 book. <u>I was dumbstruck I was just dumbstruck</u>, you painted = invented these OPAQUE-WHITE flowers these little balls of snow on the tipped-open window, the clouds the crowns of the trees like May blossoms in your lap &c., in the Cologne Lowland, in the Rhine Valley it is warmer than up here in the mountains—well I mean, a few degrees warmer, back then the willow branches with their leaves, hanging down, as the deep night descended, I thought in my soul (in Venice) that the deep night had descended then we hiked down the Iron Hand and rested in a sm. village inn, they almost smothered me those bouquets, I heard your voice but you were not there, I mean I actually heard your voice as you opened the door, I was wingèd, you were my only consolation .... I was muddled and agitated, "Bella!" he said as we parted, it was last May when I thought, "Now no more snow will fall." The thinking-system <u>of the girls</u>, namely (24.2), as the GRASS WRITING rained into my mind .... <u>nothing but chimeras</u>, you say, and look at me for a long time, while I am reading this book by Gertrude Stein I hear the voice of my deceased doctor, I hear her voice behind me from a sm. cyclone. And as I am reading your letters there appears to me this frozen BOUQUET = frozen nightingale, it was February the doe hare deceased the verses washed away from the manuscript pages. The autumn Adonis bloody in the gauze of tears in the deep heart of the woods, sometimes we shrieked through the park <u>like opaque white</u>, do you remember, those frozen bouquets, frozen nightingale &c., the pattern <u>of the dress</u> that she wore was like the <u>plumage</u> of a young cuckoo next to us in Café Sperl, 1 *youngster* in a gray vest was reading an e-book. Improvised left eye glittering, I say, or so, angel wings, what is underway there, the Thaya made speed, I say, in the twilight &c., whereas the prose sequences made me thirst to write poems, I say, doe hare that in the corner, ach, doe hare in the corner of the kitchen tableau, each morning I was excommunicated, &c., and raced every second to the typewriter, wrote 1 few words, yesterday you said, that time on a hill in Tuscany when we experienced the trance of nature OR SO : experienced the beauty of the olive gardens in the valley, left eye GLITTERING : marvelously glittering as if it held a crystal : maybe it is the uncried tears, I say, Excuse me, but are you Juliette Gréco? someone asked me on the street, behind the white rose of the ear : your ear : I hid my sm. head, I have to cry so much because I'm so happy I am the happiest person in the world .... Ann Cotten dear Ann Cotten I want to read you I'm hungry for your poems, childhood's jargon I have plumage like a young cuckoo. I was dumbstruck I was just dumbstruck as the pink Lilienthal teacup slipped, from my hand, the pink Lilienthal teacup fell to the floor : BURST. Sound like a death knell, THIS ALPENGLOW slipped from my hand &c., my darling, didn't we want, with those white bushes and swallows .... thought-film long since torn am muddled and agitated, 4–8 : I washed away the verses ach the weal (if you look at it in the MAGNIFYING GLASS &c.)"

26.2.13

"with wolf's tongue. Sweet-smelling white rose, sweet, your, ear, scenic friend I mean un-thin "un-dapper" back then, magnolia bush = masturbation early summer (Döbling next to Döblinger Hospital = Saarplatz etc.), Ann Cotten, dear Ann Cotten, I want to read your poems I want to copy them : I drew your likeness on the bed-sheet with a felt-tip pen and you said "I'm lying next to you now, near your heart, n'est-ce pas," I washed away verses, <u>am just dumb-struck</u> .... as the pink lily teacup slipped out of my hand the pink lily teacup fell to the floor and burst &c., it sounded like a death knell : "GLAS" by JD, I'm a childlet of Jesus have donned the cuckoo's feather-dress &c., and behind the white rose of the ear : of your ear, I hid my head. Glittering, the left eye, as though it held a gemstone, yesterday you said "that time, do you remember?" but I didn't remember "that time, on a hill in Tuscany when we experi-enced the trance of nature, that is, we witnessed the beauty of the olive gardens, glittering, the left eye, as though it held a crystal or perhaps it is uncried tears," I say, this alpine happiness, occurred to me : this alpenglow. These thoughts of continuation, feelings of continuation, she had one flirtation after the next : wore the pearl hen's plumage on her body .... we confided in each other, it is so magical, I say, <u>that you are so in the know</u> in my neighborhood, you know, frozen bouquet, this frozen nightingale, doe hare deceased. To my rainbird as to yours, when in spring rain falls ach when it lets its strophes sound down from tree and bush &c., am like the long-since melted snow, am a forgotten German genius flying from one tree or bush to another, not to withhold the experience of holiness of these birds, that their wings : I mean that wings grew on them so that they might give us an inkling of the existence of angels, e.g. .... now you will soon put on the red, I say, shoes, the little yellow bird on your cheek, the silver cloud on your brow, the black-crested tit which will swing on your eye &c., now you will soon put the mourning dove on your earlobe which will whisper to you the secret of spring, the sweet-smelling white rose = sweet, your ear (swan equals fawn equals gone : on Kärtnerstrasse, bought the sm. swan)

maybe pointillism, you know, this art of writing as if dabbed on, so, the snow's most recent moments &c., what a development, I say, namely wanting to spend my final years in silence and prayer, which, perhaps, made some people find me ridiculous &c. (that's pretty, it glitters so, the cap glitters so, synergetic, ach ethno-kisses oleander leotard of the moon) half-lying on the kitchen chair, watching the stars rise ...."

1.3.13

"in the morning I rinse, the depressions out of my eyes, then I sit on the kitchen chair and think, of you. The shadow of a bird tore, the curtain, the parents were full of sorrow I was, the only child. September nineteenthirty = 1st day of school, the school director pulled me onto his lap and asked me do you already know how to read. What kind of child was I : timid, blue eyes : I don't recall. Summers, we drove to the country : a courtyard, a well, the large blossoms of the elderberry trees lining the street, with bare feet down to the brook <u>to the foxes</u>, I mean periwinkle and bluebells the white longing of the hollyhocks and the lilies, and in the grass the fire salamander = regal .... I wish everyone would just get along, says Edith S.,

> (I don't like the flute <u>and Erich Kästner, fie!</u>
> Ach these birdlets, with the new, songs, I have
> strewn field flowers on your bed, I kiss your
> tresses ....)

we shrieked through the park. It seemed to me as though the bird floating over me : was a sm. angel-figure now soon you will put on the red shoes, the yellow birdlet on your hand, the low cloud on your brow, the crested lark on your eye, the mourning dove on your ear which whispers of spring .... hair still damp, left eye still tearing <u>what are those, fairy tales!</u> Night glimmers dear friend ¼ to 4 in the morning, I throw my arms around the neck of humanity, I write to Ann Cotten : I'm reading you I'm copying your poems, the full moon nips the evening star <u>then I smoke dope in the wee hours, can't sleep</u>. We shriek through the park like Easter lambs on March 3 at 8 o'clock in the morning 1 violet-blue sky, I lit up my past, we resemble communicating vessels, you know. Something comes to me, how I almost gave up the ghost,

("I'm in Tirol (Meran) am AJAX good night and hopping, in the cherry tree from branch, to branch ....")

such an arhythmical poem could almost make you shudder,"

3.3.13

"the aesthetics of the unsightly," I say, "now surely no more snow will fall," seventh of March. Someone in the dream was waving 1 white sheet once per second to show that they had surrendered, this story why was it fed to me in the dream—I mean this thought was far from my mind, or was it? would I, in the ACHING-, in the WAKING-STATE surrender to some enemy? I think, so. I react in the dream just as I would in the waking state : the same masquer-ade, arduousness, in taking action, but also rabidity ambition vanity (I mean, do you just get your actors off the street always just lay-people who've never studied acting &c., but then I said to you, he, P.H., bled from his nose for the longest time, that means, you said, he, P.H., had a NOSEBLEED, to which I repeated, he, P.H., has been bleeding from his nose for the longest time, etc. ....), the neighbor, 1 tailor, always made little repairs to his clothes for him and was also helpful in the garden, pruning his trees while hanging in the branches namely in early spring, &c. These speech-Apen-nines, you say, a bottle's graceful shoulder .... my life ach this fruitless rosebush, the next season ensued without comment : 1 intimate spring etc. .... you are my everything as we wander over the deserted grounds of the NASCHMARKT, dead-sister, yellow tennis ball under the wardrobe &c., now I am doing minimalism, I kissed you in prose, the yg. pharmacist with the neck of a spring flower, fond glances. One of my father's aunts was called "grape aunt," she was from Gumpoldskirchen, she owned a vineyard, ach Egyptian : people multiply themselves until one of the children is 1 male sprout &c., yes. Flowering plant. Soon it will be April, ten-derest month with so many tears, I have tinkered around with my life, 1 shadow falls on my mind when you. When that black swan with wide-open jaws chased us, in deepest woods and eyne of the flowers, lady-of-the-snows in B., taking the lamb to heart = I need a contemplative life (wearing rabbit fur on my skin, "I scarfed it down" = youth jargon, ES), ampersand out of the tube, two-toned Mary's tears, I'm going back to the 1930s since I am a tame forest animal, aren't I, miscellaneous pills, at night, I say, site of the flowering plant, what sweet ears you have, I show you my naked face, "this is the death knell of a pissoir," JD. Well I mean, I noticed that access to easily comprehensible things seemed denied to me so situations that I used to immediately grasp and resolve remained closed off, I mean the Thaya, rushed along like green adages (as not since time immemorial) &c., cherry blossom cited, Mother consecrated with Albinoni .... ach the spring you know with its exalted footnotes : primroses and violets pleated, blades of grass, possibly 1 mystery in these zones : private buds writings and AMAZON. Jesus Maria such an alpine face, and earlier, lovely alpine braids <u>cut</u>, mostly you plaited my fingers into long braids when we SUMMERS in the garden, and the barberry bushes bowing over our heads : <u>evermore</u> as the evening-shine, gesture of splendor,

10.3.13

"I'm <u>your chick</u> or doll il giardino in
your eyes ach in the guildhall of my illu-
sions &c."

"just to sit somewhere and brood sometimes,

looking for Goethe's notebooks"

„ich brenne –.....

["I'm burning ...."]

12.3.13

"the yellow hair of the women by Picasso, you are 1 symbol, I love you very much, ach the early spring you know with its encrypted footnotes, its cryptic primroses and violets might be a simile most silken zones with pink buds exalted writings and AMAZON, I enclosed 1 teardrop in a letter to you, namely Satie's who floated me away, well actually, declaimed the bushes .... "do inspect the buds of the apricot tree, madame," we tumbled into Libro Café &c., since the fragile calls of the mountain cuckoo circa, violet and pennywort in the depths of the garden, ach with thorns, needle-apparitions, the course of time, autumn Adonis veiled, namely, in the wild heart of the woods, gauze of tears of your, disposition, : 1 borrowed term, isn't it. This layperson of the wood-shadows back then this trophy of the muddy ground around the lake, while the scab and the bounciness of the veins, namely, kitchen-lamento, night-glimmers dear friend ½ past 3 in the morning I hid my head behind the white rose of your ear, mostly my poems are a-logical, I mean the hoisting of a thought, for example, like when Valérie B. says to me that when she was little she was afraid to look at her own navel .... evermore, over our heads this resurgence of the seasons, he fondled the garden. 1 small door : what was I supposed to, GLOWERING, meanwhile he forgot to translate "unlit," smell of fish in the morning. 1 teardrop enclosed in a letter to you, calligra-phied the Thaya, these speech-Apennines, and shrieked through the park like Easter lambs. While the bounciness of the blackbird, I say, while the room of tears, he called out JESUS MARIA and threw the rotting fruit .... yes. Flowering plant, I kissed you in prose, dead-sister tennis ball, and Father often said, "I could care LESS, etc.," now I'm a minimalist. When we had long since ceased to do it. I'm addicted to you, ach saucy sun, since she lamented : motherlet : world-soul, the globe is SHEDDING NEEDLES, like my old dried-out Christmas tree, almost Easter already and I'm still freezing, 1 batch of tears, you say, I need the thrill. 1 flower-,1 fountain-bouquet (a bit debonair) &c., "moro, lasso" = "I'm dying, ach" (1611). Ach, yesterday : a fool made of my form, as we stood entwined : overhead the chestnut buds, tears in my eye, in my left eye sm. cloths flying past, claviature of the conifers .... I was still small I was afraid to look into my own navel, said Valérie B., I found 1 claw in a flock of fur, and Ely was flying toward me. As if I would approach the fire with my last embroidered countenance, ach write only the impossible, you say, whereupon I spread out my arms, point to the snowballs (fleurs?) and call "heat! : heart!," and we fell in love with our erstwhile lives, your quiet insistence .... I have gone to seed : as though I were flying, 1 drop of blood fell on the snow, &c."

14.3.13

"*winter my lovely*" .... at a certain point one can't go on and just wants to sleep. Heinz Schafroth, 81, classical philologist, here my farewell, he pressed my hand, "that you're here," he said, "that you are writing, makes me glad." Adieu adieu blackthorn-hued your soul where has it gone, "ach, write only the impossible," you say, as though you were flying (sm. Swiss pine) : 1 drop of blood fell on the snow, namely, it chimed like a death knell = "GLAS" by Jacques Derrida. Once in the middle of Vienna on the GRABEN as we parted : I accompanied you to the descent into the U-Bahn, and as you sank into the depths I waved to you, while you glided down the escalator you glided down, that time, the teardrop = mourning dove on your brow .... well I mean, there was crackling in the woods, and when you looked out at Lake Biel the waves of the lake glittered such that the sun-wildernesses scalded your delicate eyes. Possibly a mystery in these zones,

14.3.13

"ach, pilgrimage voice *"winter my lovely."* You are my everything as we go along <u>swept-clean blackbird in NY</u>, 1 "SO-TO-SPEAK" with a bite taken out of it, namely squashed tomato, and Morse codes, you say, "debaucheries" : Jean Paul, and then we go ice skating .... my left eye is weak it tears up and leaks out &c. when we don't see each other for 1 day I feel excluded, 1 loner 1 lone wolf let's say, <u>1 screamer, I scream into 1 bouquet</u>, you know, EMACIATION, you know, isolation, you know, a <u>listener-to-records</u>, <u>walker-around</u> in a park &c., flambéed Phantasus, you know, everything's imaginary. Back then before the cloudburst as we ran to the restaurant for cover, I mean argot-language, I kissed you, in prose, yes. Flowering plant. Soon April tenderest month with tears, <u>after we had long since ceased to do it</u> .... 1 shadow falls on my mind, ach yesterday a fool of my innermost form, <u>ach claviature of the conifers</u>, my little Christmas tree has shed its needles, 1 flurry of blessings, perhaps 1 new wave of Romanticism is upon us, 1 fume of pink, chirping cicada in my ear = am protégée, sitting on the salvia chair, the full moon (pours) its gloria into the profound valley, the end is dispelled : expelled .... we have forgotten much, for our life was very long. In my navel 1 mini bouquet of SCHIKANEDER, you know, cluster of blossomsnow, am sitting by the window. And as if AS a morning prayer, still lying = huddling in bed, I tend to read, although my eyes keep getting weaker especially the left one. My bedsheet all scratched up in the colors of the rainbow (with felt-tip pen) .... when no notebook was to hand &c., now I'm even drawing your stately figure on the headrest = or, lying on the sofa I remember the days we lay together on the bed NESTLED into each other <u>extricating the sun from the sky</u> I mean like a blanket <u>or fading enclosure</u>, as a yg. person I <u>scribbled</u> a lot, in fact I have very much gone to seed, you know (16.3), my nightgown torn and BLOTTED and sometimes it seems to me : the more I let myself go the bolder my imagination becomes, how can that be? I write often to Georg W., although I have nothing to report : 1 compulsion : I don't really understand it …….. ach sapphire-blue and asters, am sitting on the salvia chair, wandering around in a park, &c., I mean the dawning day, ach your quiet insistence, because the sweet pennyworts under the garden chairs WERE ACTUALLY TEEMING, like Frauenfeld, the air however evermore sclerotic, to doubt, to take one example. Today a bit of queasiness, daymoon-pallid my mood &c., you are my only solace, ach these asseverations, I go into döner shops, don't think much of "political correctness" especially in connection with linguistic aspects, I intend each morning to visit the ALBERTINA where right now there's a big Max Ernst exhibition, I mean, I am a protégée. Well, was it the scent of the hyacinths or the touch-me-nots that was wafting : wandering : diffusing through the writing room, there was a Sardinian student asking me questions about poetry which I, however, was unable to answer. The skeleton of the little Xmas tree had shrieked, we swayed through the city center past the DOROTHEUM, and meanwhile the pink moon nearly lacerated my heart. I have a sweet tooth, sometimes, I always provoked the same phrases, I mean the text frolicked …….."

16.3.13

"ach swept-clean blackbird in NY, Jesus on Lazarus : "he already smells," I will visit you, I can't see well, the lark, ach listening-to-records walking-around-in-a-park &c., 1 garçon 1 early bird 1 Ajax I knocked on your door but you wouldn't open to me, there was just, in the darkness, your gleaming eyes, I barged into your flower-eyes I drowned in your beautiful flower-eyes, am 1 screamer I scream into 1 bouquet, you know, when you lead me by the hand, you know, everything's 1 hymen : 1 symbol. Everything's so imaginary, isn't it, I kissed you in prose, yes. Flowering plant = had disgorged, stem broke off (hyacinth) : pink, fragrant, 1 shadow falls on my mind, "you played as if toward heaven," said Boccherini, am protégée, I have a sweet tooth sometimes, the chirping flower-gowns hang in the four winds while dark-blue hour of dawn because these forest-chords .... the cuckoos namely, as if I were smitten, that's how my INDUSTRIOUSNESS leads me to new works. Am protégée sitting on the salvia chair, the ruching namely of the Baltic Sea, I burn, amid an unfathomable sea, of flowers, feverishly dispersed butterflies ach we sank into the cabbage whites .... as we sat in the little garden in Rome, the noble matrons passed us by in their black gowns with their little black purses. Mother never wore earrings, but then after Father's death she started sticking clip earrings on her earlobes, yes, I remember for all the world I wanted to go on that reading tour, even if it would make her cry, must you, go on this trip? as if I were daydreaming, it consumed me, swans of spring, thrush in apple tree, I wake up with blissfulness and NODULE of earth, don't I, my little Lena, my little sword, we sat in the upper garden, theory of the disenchanted world, "eye and hand fevering after the unself" (Beckett) .... it's only March but they're already building this road through our garden, she said back then, you know, the sea ROLLS, you know, in dark undulations, how the sea rolls up to your feet and over mountain and valley your path and past the olive trees the wisteria woods and bougainvillea, you know, the lianas lilies lilting cypresses by the sea-strand .... you are alone (pressure marks of love, n'est-ce pas), dark clouds, leaning at the window no moon and no stars, but the rod BLOSSOMED in the sand, ach they take you into their arms it is like 1 weeping, and I screwed up my courage &c., you're a soy-child you're a rainbow as if I'd been smitten, touch-me-not nosegay at your breast, you bit into the flower-heads, shoved your locks over your eyes so that the DESERT light would not blind you. And no flowery language, the rosemary is blooming, you know, the storks are brooding on the steeple .... (denticles of the asters how you quivered, locks and LOERKE, on my cheek a little bump = little globule of earth, you know, reign, my heart,)"

18.3.13

"am a bit theatrical in the morning, the ruching of the Baltic Sea, namely the PARK-SITTERS, deep-blue morning hour, and then you have defeated your eye gauze. Little bump little nodule where MAMA went, she didn't dare go out on the street she was ashamed before the PARK-SITTING-ONES she rushed past them although her silk scarf did protect = envelop her 1 little she was lost to herself back then, little bump little nodule of earth, where MAMA went &c. .... monstrous crouching namely I am ignited, the bitter honey (like a droplet of blood) on my fingertips, in the morning, I mean, I recall something = I am called once more, I say, namely a re-collecting, or I can't recollect something that happened yesterday : what happened yesterday, where did Ann Cotten's verses go, possibly blooming in a cornerlet of the room, can't find them, oh well, I mean, I gave my blessing to her poems and vice versa, till I almost died of delectation so I started to spoon it with my finger, almost spooned up the bitter honey with my finger. A bit like rum and cordial, and in the kitchen like dying hyacinths .... sun : frontman of the clouds, back then in Ossiach where you detected Wally's shadow in the bushes a few days before he died, so green and liquid the landscape, so aromatic the cliffs the herbs the moonlight. Ever more language slips my mind as though I were 1 little Xmas tree shedding needles (to Candlemas = February 2 and the Christmas trees went up in flames I mean they blazed, so was I, shedding needles, was wordless, Feuchtersleben as a stripling, JESUS MARIA, am I reactionary, or what. And profligate am I when before the SINKING sun, something comes to me) .... 1 illusion the pink vetch on the fences and I'm singing in the wood-shadow, I mean Alban Berg : "did you see the forest after the thundershower?" &c. And nibbling the wood-beauty, I hang on your lips. The little bell of the clitoris, the term "scare quotes" on my tongue,

EMACIATION, you know, a fool of my form, isolation : listening-to-records, <u>walking-around in a park &c.</u>, argot-language, flambéed Phantasus, everything's imaginary, &c., sometimes I provoked : always the same phrases that I write down, in my left eye : always these little cloths flying by, touchscreen, of an unthinkable sea, we were sitting in the little upper garden, ach my darling shall we enchant the world once more? a few seconds before one is completely awake : state of oscillation .... <u>no flowery language</u> : am a little Xmas tree shedding needles and bare, in my meadows are no more stars, I say, well, since I woke up in the snow of my dreams there were these persistent dry stems flowing toward me I'd like to recall a certain parallel : but it is extinguished at the very moment I want to note it down .... memory blitzes namely, next to me 1 bent bare nape of a no-longer-quite-so-young woman (like italitá) = allée of nut trees : fascinating in profile her classic stage-eye, a female Goethe, say. Later in the imperative, no flowery language the fuming Easter fire, the more so as it wafted away into the lowest valley (this object that almost fell down, so, e.g., a <u>swallow</u> = album atilt, to let oneself fall is something like gentle feathers in my eyes or the smile of the yellow down duvet in the morning, the divine fold .... oh how we will drowse, while the budding landscape). I walked over to the GALS in the hair salon to have my black bangs <u>snipped</u>, bit of a twinge in my left breast. Fatuous and at night the pine trees on that photo P.H. sent me .... moonlight over Cycladic island"

24.3.13

"violet-wise. Hydrangea, firelet in my breast, now you will soon put on the new red shoes, well actually, it was the hair-dryer workshop that blew such hot air on my chest .... to bed. In the <u>firmament</u> the Sacred Heart also the little lilac tree trunk where the PARK-SITTERS, it was because there were no drinking glasses in the hospital that I drank from my left hand, I let the water <u>trill</u> from the faucet (how happy I was to have found this word, wasn't I, what a beautiful word : I let it TRILL, ach Joseph Maria), so the water <u>trilled</u> from the faucet : the Genet-, the Ponge-aria I mean the Genet-, the Ponge-tradition and suchlike. I let the drinking water from the faucet <u>trill</u> over my left hand as if I were ladling it from a village well : from a mountain spring, and I drank out of my left hand what a delectation, wasn't it, and I wrote on a green <u>winged folder</u> while the swallow visited me with her opened <u>pinions</u> while the pearls of the dawn teemed before my eyes .... it was astounding, I dreamed of a handful of cooked fish, and instead of in a little bowl, I handed them to you, I handed them over to you, in the little bowl of my hand, the more so as in the lowest valley the little lilac tree trunks had poetic last names, they were named "Firmament" and "Volcano" and "Sensation" (the thing I'd been looking for all over was right in front of my eyes, but I didn't see it) .... yesterday I <u>bestirred</u> myself to a walk along the edge of the woods and I saw the first pennyworts which made me think of the HELENENTAL valley, I also had to immediately think of you, later very impulsively the pale little curls in the dream <u>also urge to urinate</u>, my white tennis shoes = *sneakers*, and everything so TRUE TO LIFE in my dream : presumably blackberry hedge (ach Mama : presumably snake-patch, I said to you "we should go to the Drechsler again sometime &c."), ach no flowery language, the storks are already brooding. Of an unthinkable heart,

you say, very much gone missing .... however much I take DEEP
BREATHS tomorrow morning, I might keep writing poems <u>unto</u>
<u>dizziness</u>, clivia. Of an unthinkable heart, you call out, whereas the
budding landscape whereas fatuous and at night, a bit heavenward
so that my soul-wings will want to grow again, you know, almond-
eyed spring, gloriette of the morning, yes Beloved, I slept with no
thought for tomorrow while your little body in the shower
WHOLLY IN PINK, in the afternoon .... just no heel spurs! in
the Maria-Joseph Park (blue park), the auricle namely (30.3), the
holding-fast to a word in the moment of awakening, <u>shmatte e.g.</u>,
gladiola-sword .... I mean she spoke on the phone about an inti-
mate experience little notes of birds / screwing in the lavatory &c.
well I mean, I couldn't keep any secrets, could keep nothing to
myself, had to blab everything, you know, GROANING is
GREENING, "single tree and betrothed trees," Max Ernst, 1940,
<u>my wincing</u> ...."

30.3.13

"Night glimmers dear friend, ½ past 3 in the morning, teardrop enclosed in a letter to you, 31st of March now surely no more snow will FALL (aesthetic of the absurd) Philipp Hössli writes "withering bouquets I washed myself with Bettina, ach, dried my hands, donned my red-silk bolero, and then for a long time we stayed close to each other" .... something comes to me, this time while writing I didn't cry, you know, these tender associations Apulias, in an awake life-state the wingbeat of an eyeblink, the wingbeat of the years, a bunch of gingko boughs branchlets leaflets (bolero) woven into a wreath, I'm hunting chasing lusting after a certain book : now I'm chasing lusting hunting for a certain book and cannot stop, Goethe tended, in his writings, to use abbreviations. Somewhat stormy, you say, 1 nature trail. You say, and if it should never be spring again, we're sitting in the Rüdigerhof, how I do love you, it seemed to me as though 1 object had rolled off the tabletop I mean there was 1 vague noise 1 blue pencil, from my innermost body, the teardrops rolled. The devotional meadow, he says, my shadowiest wife &c. Upon waking, on my tongue "BROWN BETTY" .... they treat me like 1 child, the auricle the groaning the thorn-branches the bosque in the forest aisle "single tree and betrothed trees" Max Ernst 1940, Beckett's "wincing," firelet in my breast, holding fast to a word in the moment of awakening, "shmatte" e.g., undaunted the 1st buds in the park &c., the ants in the WC, "got lost walking with X," &c., on your little foot the word CRETE while the grains of sand on my tongue n'est-ce pas, haunted at night FATUOUS on the dais, and I applauded into her (Mother's) prayers with my paws, your locks smelling of tobacco, I was magnetized, we liked best to sit on the dais at the Rüdigerhof, violet-wise your innermost dreams .... if anything were to befall you : I would die. The waxy orchids = auricles, in my fist, the thorn-branches, Philipp Hössli's diary entries 1821–24, you inflamed me, it is long past midnight my eyes dry and sleepless (no *movie* April 3), my lips prayered to rawness in the night, I covered my face with my hands and let my innermost films go by, I'm AJAX and good night. Little nightbird in the cherry tree hopping from branch to branch, <u>I want to go shopping for swallows : CD, in the city</u>, oh how we will drowse .... ach I roam around circa had phantasies of violet and pennywort in the depths of the garden, the laic : the wood-shadow : back then the trophy from the muddy ground on the overpass around the lake, I mean one would need 1 MODEL : 1 TEMPLATE : to have SOMETHING COME TO ONE, you know, and tracks one can enter : can jubilate like mountain cuckoos ("Do inspect the mountain cuckoo's fragile calls, madame, &c.") .... namely 1st chartreuse delusion or glimmer of the Little Weather Book : forsythia bush : frontman of early spring, glimpsed in the distance. In whose footprints one can walk, &c."

3.4.13

"ach the moon, keeping me company .... measuring the light masses of a landscape I mean photographic dreams of a landscape of pleasurable whirling = wind of a pear tree which was decorated with 1 little bird, photocopied edge of the woods = "but we did go there 1 x!" silvery drapery of a sky, echo of an incessant premises .... write or stride in the bright early springtide, lurching loop lane through the lea : there, we entered. Giant palms as milestones, in a painting by Max Ernst namely "single tree and betrothed trees" with *sneakers* .... thirsting for a bona fide source in P. = etui of a summer night &c., back then with E. who was leaning <u>against 1 boscage</u>, confidant, without speaking, <u>and a tatterlet of feeling</u> : that's just 1 tick, you say, those apostrophes : raining or dewing "*sweet April.*" On a wan morning from the window : <u>distorted Schönbrunn</u> &c., and with wide-open eyes = eyelets Rachmaninoff's Prelude in C Sharp Minor that time, and cried into it namely chartreuse delusion or drowse. Thirring spoke of the "dear moon" &c., in the end he spoke, Thirring, of the "dear moon" which at the right distance from Earth, n'est-ce pas, in the <u>bushy distance</u> ach the company of my beloved = the moon, Bettina's thorn-branches, firelet in my breast listening to Rachmaninoff's Prelude in C Sharp Minor, &c., tatterlet of feeling : waxy orchids in my fist, the eyne of the flowers, on your bedsheet scribbled "Wind on the Plain" (Debussy), later in the imperative. Your black locks. Something comes to me, the pine trees namely, a bit heavenward ach so that the wings will want to grow on me once more, tomorrow morning .... (Morandi's jugs), you know, wreaths of poppies on Mother's grave &c., and in Mother's kitchen, on the windowsill the bath cartridges, the asparagus, the fieldfare, ach, she said, the many flowers and ornaments .... your eyes full of longing ("le kitsch") and shrieking through the park like Easter lambs, then I smoke a joint near morning, can't sleep. Which aggrieves her, she says, like grievous weather (grief) : it might stay like that until June, no?—<u>blew out one</u>

of the words in the most fiery of meadows, like a candle .... it has all taken a turn for the worse : I'm afraid of a silverfish : I feel pursued by silverfishes in the bathroom, I mean the dear tears (flow) I mean the procession of dear tears, etc., it's enough, we have reached the point where we turn around : there was this paraphrase : passage : passion : this passing of the Stubenring by his (H.H.'s) side, when he said "my little dove is worried about me," he said that, you know, but he didn't kiss me goodbye before he got out, presumably it would have been too intimate ("this book wants to be just 1 tiny slice of my inner life," JD), so I struggled up the steep staircase, namely, the lyre, my feet hurt. Well, the picture of a saint trimmed with lace that I fished out of the backpack, you say, I forgot a lot, I say, much has plunged into the depths of my consciousness. It was a winter day and I was slinking past the large window of Café Rathaus in which you were sitting, and I imagined that I (. . .) your head behind the windowpane, then I wrote everything down, but you took a pair of scissors and cut your wool scarf, I mean, a circumcision. A slitting-open of your feelings, wasn't it. As we climbed up through the bosquets of the spa garden I mean reading all the letters on a bench in the spa garden, climbing up the withering bosquets : of calla lilies, of orchids, of hyacinths, forget-me-nots .... could it be that the red felt-tip pen had simulated the fatal hemorrhage on my white pajama pants, which made me gasp, &c., suspicious pants and thesaurus too, slitting-open of that shared train ride, at some point it will be over, I mean we will have reached a point at which you can no longer SUCCOR me, I mean, it will be beyond your strength, won't it, FAT LADY / SANG, well I mean, your future is bleeding, you say, we go to see the Max Ernst exhibition in the Albertina. Like a tuft of grass, I say, MOORED in your soul, "Madame, do you believe in the afterlife?"........"

7.4.13

nicht vergessen !

don't forget!

"opera buffa : inundation at the breakfast table 40 drops of Oleovit
D$_3$ from the pipette, diary entries of Philipp Hössli (1821–24) : 100
years before I alighted from paradiso, in my eyes, water, in the
clouds, flocks, ach they dive into the deeps, they charge into the
heights, oh, how free they are. Riven my heart, broken my bones
my 1st thought in the morning, you know, is you, I mean that yel-
low meadow full of dandelions and as the 3 of us sat in the car I
could feel myself DAFFODILING, etc., I mean that dandelion
meadow that could (. . .) your heart, &c., I saw that most years,
while the secret, I mean April breeze, secret spring moon &c. and
now when the yellow meadows full of dandelions begin to glow, I
have seen it for so many years now, one never believed that the
winter would really end, until suddenly it did, with the first birdlet
—and then one forgot all over again. This conception, I mean as
far as my beloved mother is concerned : was she still as young as a
springtime morning when he, my beloved father, planted this
embodiment of me in her : sm. holy reservoir in which the bud was
embedded .... ach the PARK-SITTERS, you know, in the
ascending dawn : ascending absconding dawn : ferry of the airs :
flower of the oleander pure of heart, darling cataracts of withering
blossoms, ach the spring with its encrypted footnotes : cryptic prim-
roses and violets of private writings buds and AMAZON, allegory
of the pink tongue : something comes to me .... exalted basket
of cherries in the back courtyard &c., unspeakable these beautiful
days with you, you say, and so I half-wanted this, half-wanted that,
I broke off in the middle, exquisite imagistic language, you say, cig-
arette in the morning, embushed you say, a sudden torrent of words,
a bit refreshed, you say, moored in your soul, waxy orchids in my
fist, Gennady Aygi died c. 8 years ago, middle aunt how she looks
at me, livid, and says, "your blue eyes, &c." Malapropism of life,

gone for a ride : luminaries : these firs, sycamores, darling cataracts of white withering blossoms .... am a ruin, a drop of urine : pretty much most audacious formulations and meanwhile we <u>lovebird to lovebird</u> you know, ach we went to Café Jelinek the writing blazed as if I were daydreaming or as Gory Graham says "MARRY INTO" and she asked me if I had heard 1 invention on Jacques Derrida on the radio &c. In the stone that you brought me back from Crete, I say, the sea had etched itself with dancing foot &c. "And I hate, even in novels, all the storytelling so much" (Jean Paul) .... shimmering tin camel on the bed, the Thaya made speed, suddenly I'm exhausted : I lay my head to the right, fall asleep again in the late morning, little birds were whirring around as I awakened, weren't they, dainty alpine flowers, we turned around : the mountains were shrouded. But no, said MAMA, even if you take the sleeping-powder you will wake back up. Repetitions of a dream, look! the grandmother, we did want to buy a new mattress, someone said to B., "you look like 1 fertility goddess" .... I can still see it now, 13 years later, how the two of you came out of the elevator up here on the 5th floor and <u>flung your arms around me</u> : your condolence visit &c. it was a day like today I mean 1 radiant afternoon, through the corridor window, and <u>we flung our arms around each other</u> and cried. Like (climbing) out of the bath I climbed out of my dream this morning and began immediately .... AS IF IN INFIDELITY .... I felt a gobbet of phlegm and spat it into my nightgown and then I found myself in the thick of the action, the pain started up again, 1 green veil before my eyes, <u>the little particle</u> "you know" lends the whole thing 1 certain intimacy, you say, I note with half-closed eyes, we were wearing face masks, I mean today you will not visit me <u>through the tall grasses</u>, it was 1 gorgeous yellow April morning, I gasped when I saw my face in the mirror. We ambled along the edge of the <u>Naschmarkt</u>, the tall Mediterranean potted plants were adjusted into place, we sat in the "Drechsler" and observed that .... well I mean, bidding or begging in Café Sperl with a banknote in my hand I sat down next to the bar pianist on the bench and asked him, may I give you this banknote, oh yes, he had already hurried past our booth earlier tossing out greetings &c. I spat into my nightgown, this remained lodged in my memory also the lilac occurrence of an Easter gathering as MAMA suddenly got out or rolled out of the shuddering car, namely, on that Easter Sunday and everything LILAC ("le kitsch") &c., well I mean, on the edge of the bed the little ash-rose, n'est-ce pas, it was already 8"

16.4.13

"today you will not visit me through the tall grasses, a tiny just-hatched fly on the frame of the window opened a crack I coaxed her with a piece of paper to liberty but she cowered, she was frightened, so I let her be. Whereas 1 pink (baroque) cloud in the east, rumbling, and I thought, birds are the freest creatures of all .... red flower of the oleander pure of heart, I see him how he stood before me in a white jacket back then, in Bad Ischl, this year I took the 1st violets to the Central Cemetery : sweet violet and I read the names of the dead from the gravestones, I read out the names under my breath, then pressed the Easter basket with the yellow spring-time flowers against the headstone. Since the spring was WATER UNDER THE BRIDGE you know, I built waterworks &c. This spring is pretending to be 1 summer (with sharp tongue), so said you, that is, so said you very near my ear, it was 1 whisper and you plunged deep into my eyes and your eyes were 2 blue flowers that wafted before me : that's how it went straight to my heart while the allée of hornbeams &c. in endless devotion, ach like humming fruits of the whole world .... my stilt-like legs. I was perplexed, when I wanted to continue reading the book I turned the page, but there weren't any more words, the text stopped in the middle of a sentence (like Jacques Derrida's "Glas" &c.), "I almost died of inflammation," to lust after this e.g. in the forest, in the wingèd corner, age is 1 little ash-rose, ach your blitz-capability, yes Beloved, I sleep as though there were no tomorrow, I approach stealthily in your dreams, I copy the day's coloring from you. Lying on my sofa I remembered the time when together we .... listened to Forqueray &c., droning moonlight. God-commended Adorno the sm. pink watering can in the kitchen we extol the spring rains, the withered cryptic primrose bouquet in the glass (23.4) or the little withering primrose bouquet's colors faded &c. listening to

Forqueray, ach invisible, my sensorium sharp-eyed = sharp-tongued .... ANUS torn, as once in childhood : the rough winters and the sweet springs. Sweetpea's tears between violet's tears on the cemetery lawn I awaken at 3 in the morning and say to myself, I am alone, "all typewriters," ach such somnambulist times, gloriette of the morning that everything, EVEN my heart, breaks, Friedl Kubelka cries her eyes out, she takes her upper teeth out, makes us lemonade, like an adored shadow the image of my mother in old age pursues my days and nights : I carry it within me and now I am becoming it so that EVEN my heart broke, &c. I mean : blazed : when standing before the sinking sun "I almost died of inflammation" .... dreamed I read maundered in Jean Paul, the writing blazes, so green and liquid landscape, in my Apulia, in the wingèd corner (we devour time, and time devours us) .... as for the Café Jelinek, it is 1 jaws of hell, you know"

23.4.13

"pure of heart this cataract of white blossoms. In the wingèd corner of the north face of the Eiger we all felt = in the belly of the mountain, the brush of death, &c."

for Valérie Baumann
23.4.13

"I was ravenous and then my intestines spoke to me and called me by my name so green and liquid landscape and withered beak of bushwind roselet, the writing blazes, dreamed and sighed, just like wind cajoling I laid my hand on his back, a hint of wind, then took it off again immediately &c., in my Apulia I removed my hand, feel like I'm going through withdrawals, in the trench, on the couch, in all situations, ach bel canto at the edge of the woods, in summer often like fire in the allée .... Over there, in the meadow, the 1st daffodils, deep-green grottoes, like tufts of grass. I moored in your soul, like a tuft of grass moored in your soul, you are my only sol-ace, you know, light and masses of a pleasing landscape whirl of a tall acacia tree .... rosettes and glitter : the woods that in my heart &c., without speaking to each other, tatterlet of feeling, raining or dewing "*sweet April*," a particle of mansuetude .... "God bless you, my child, you slept endlessly" (no *movie*, end of April), we sat together in the garden, the wormwood spruce, we washed together and fabulated, you read the words from my lips or pluck them from me like blackthorn from my brow, as though I were daydreaming, you know, because we are enchanted, we two. In the most luxuriant clover the bright eye-tears your swift pace, I almost died of delec-tation, Jean Paul, it haunted me, childhood reminiscences I am a childlet of Jesus I have a feather-dress = cuckoo's plumage on, I don't possess any thoughts I possess only my language : AND WITH IT I MAKE NOISE, &c., I rummaged around for you as for a little gold ring, amen yes and amen waveth the 1st sight of stars, all and sundrie and slept endlessly, because of my lust I saw (absolutely) nothing, just with the mother of god to the snow and in(to) the twilit rain .... you enflamed me it is long past midnight beloved my eyes sleepless, no *movie* April 3 "train stations are for weeping, God bless you my child you are my only solace &c.," and then I remembered that you had written me this letter months ago but I no longer knew where I had put it, and so what would I REFER BACK TO now .... in the window, ink-blue, cypress-high ecstasy : white ossicle of daybreak, well I mean, unique tears, beloved. In the kitchen 1 x the ants had disappeared, why, where'd they go? (I'm quoting EJ's "rele<u>as</u>e him" by pronouncing 1 "tee-aich" namely "relea/th (him)" <u>what 1 spectacle</u> which actually means ~~☞~~ .... what a lilac tree = resplendence what a sweet erring when I picture to myself in the morning what all we will do during the day, I mean what 1 enchantment this day lying before us &c., well I mean, in the wingèd corner 1 lilac tree as though I were daydreaming ach, Feuchtersleben as a stripling, namely ...."

25.4.13

"pansy's eye-pair I could have died, you didn't want <u>any foreplay</u>, back then, <u>ach blue dram</u> of temperaments, the pantaloons hung at the window, today 5 in the morning with SAUCER EYES I observed the colossal full moon, namely, I flinched. I told him afterward who I was (so that he wouldn't ruin the pleasantry), Constable .... my GRAMO is playing Antony, I'm enraptured, that is, <u>in the blue chasm of temperaments</u>, you say, after we were unable to see each other for a few weeks, I mean, it came to pass that we ran into each other accidentally OR SO in Café Jelinek which was 1 resplendence 1 lilac bush 1 sweet <u>errancy</u> or thought-whisper and then all morning I played the weeping Antony on the GRAMO in the wingèd corner and could have died, we washed together and you dried my hair, pure of heart this cataract of white blossoms, namely, that had withered : they blazed : Jesus Maria am I reactionary or what, you detected Wally's shadow in the lisping, I mean lisping clouds (Ossiach) after he died, didn't you .... to look at a blind man is frightening I mean to look a blind man in the eyes, as though I were a little Xmas tree to Candlemas and shedding needles : February 2 (since the Christmas trees went up in flames, I mean <u>blazed</u>, soon I was all out of words, so to speak, our gazes couldn't catch, touch each other : they stumbled around the little room, and withered beak (bushwind roselets)). <u>A bit like Rome</u>, spooned with my finger, EJ was a moralist, bushed in the morning, and, I believe, ink-blue agony &c., these mosses : sowing in the erring = rill, it haunted me .... ravenous this riven spring, ach I will be looking for you all over but I will not find you, won't find you anywhere while the flitting sun. As he kissed me that time 1 little bouquet of dew fell from his brow to my lip 1 little bouquet of dew the day was hot ("*lead me not into temptation*"). Bewildered bird-image, and as for dying, it has nothing to do with me, I say (although a ruin).

Exalted *country music* from Antony Hegarty : quite unspeakable
.... so this flock kneeled : pearls of dawn, something comes to
me (of course she spoke of EMBRACING him, so there sprang the
whole title at once : "from embracing the sparrow-wall," in our
memories again, same raining of joys and sorrows in the greenery,
mainly now I observe the bodily movements of mountains water
trees and flowers, Egon Schiele), I fan these little dream-flames,
you say, you let it all wash over you, you say, and so everything
carried on elliptically, which is to say, your language carried on
elliptically. Something hurts, and meanwhile the wind was blowing
ach the wind was blowing into the living room so, I mean mortally
wounded .... source of the wind whence the mortally wounded
wind, I mean, I don't understand it, I mean it was chained up, the
wind, but now it has torn free, I mean it blew into my face when I
opened the window, blew into your hair : a blossom-fresh blowing
wasn't it where did it come from I don't know, it hath blown : a
giant wind-instrument blew into our faces and into your tresses,
blew into your fresh face in the morning whence did it come, what
is its origin, its place of birth, can you tell me that, my friend ....
hand in hand with you, (yes) heaven on earth .... and actually
she did bring me every morning to school and 1 dove would float
over our heads, you know, and as we walked hand in hand down
the street to the "English misses" ("English" means "from the
angels") she promised me heaven on earth facing me dreamily, and
after a few hours she would pick me up from school and bring me
home : we walked hand in hand and it was 1 heaven and we loved
each other very much. Other people understood me only somewhat
but only she really understood me and she said, "you will outshine
everyone" when I lost heart, or when Margit S. teased me, and on
Christmas Eve just before the stores closed she ran down to buy

me more Christmas presents, she showered me with her love. Then she sat under the Christmas tree <u>and sat there very quietly</u> the whole evening, my parents too sat there very quietly the whole evening, until finally Father put out the candles and we went to bed. And when she died at a very old age I was not beside her because she had said "you will not know it when I die," and I did not hold her hand : she went all alone (as if I would go to the fire, with her last countenance) .... and it's 1 person the wind <u>1 cool person</u> when I put my head out the window, <u>1 person that blows &c.</u> .... because we are enchanted, my arms of unequal lengths, wanderer phantasy, the invisible Loire, you say, I saw the moon shrouding itself : 1 gauze of tears &c., "like contented love that CONSOLES our hearts" .... goldfinch at your feet (with addicted eye) pearling like tears, etc."

28.4.13

"in part I always provoked the same phrases, you know, while the swifts I mean like a black cross over the WIENZEILE, singing, cheeping, you drew my jacket tight, this writing-passion draws the writer tight, I was ravenous, and we, sauntering along the WIEN-ZEILE, along the Naschmarkt, will it be cherries / olives that end up on the kitchen floor, you ask, while over the WIENZEILE, "look, 1 swift, over the WIENZEILE," the little bouquet of bell-flowers in the glass now totally dead of thirst sucked up and drank down the last drops, *you are my lover, let's go to Australia*," and ravenously sauntered. It drove me wild ach the bellflowers, in part I provoked the same phrases, you searched through my pockets for the thermometer which I couldn't find anywhere with a sweet severity on your face as though I were your undutiful child &c. Something hurts, ravenously blew the wind through our hair, on midsummer's day while the gentle bushes BLESSED us THROUGH AND THROUGH, and back then you didn't want any foreplay : you wanted to get down to business didn't you, X. still had under-arm hair, blond. On your ring-fingernail you had a moon, on my two thumbnails I too had moons, it was very touching that X., I mean that X. still had underarm hair, blond, as she lifted her beautiful arm up to smooth her head-hair (28.4 "*high*") .... the now totally dry little bouquet of bellflowers had drunk had sucked up the last drops from the vase, something hurts, it blew, the wind through our hair, "no eyelashes anymore at all," I wore a little coat made of gold paper cf. Oskar Schlemmer's costumes for the "Triadic Ballet" &c., it drove me wild ach the bellflowers : it drove me wild because I could hear the bellflowers tolling, in the shadow of your locks, as we rode the LILLIPUT TRAIN back then, the wind blew in our hair, the green crowns of the trees .... I opened the window I heard a sound from a piano, from the

GRAMO Antony and the Johnsons, he sings like 1 hanged man, ach he laughs like 1 yg. deer &c., ach heart-on-sleeve in a trice, the long tits. I experienced 1 disgrace I let this disgrace wash over me, emotion of flowers, JD, bluetit careening with addicted eye, goldfinch at your feet welling with tears, between foxglove and coltsfoot, I only want a liquid diet, ach you laugh like 1 yg. deer &c., this was the ecstasy : as I awoke at 4 in the morning the wind blew into my WRITING ROOM and I saw everything blurred as if underwater, kneeling before this white lilac, on the lawn while the branchlets, glimmered, I frittered away 4 days and nights with slips of paper I was confused I didn't know what day it was what time, I mean in our isolation we decorated our sm. house, it was interdependencies, you know, we crushed the dark-blue tango (together) like an emptied plastic bottle, Komm lieber Mai und mache. In the morning, the impression of my skull on the pillow .... the clouds like May blossoms in the trees of the VOLKSGARTEN &c., you baptized me and I believe you can magic away my age (that is your character) .... agitated feelings, we frolicked across the swept-clean."

1.5.13

"I believe you can magic away my age, snow in my heart now no more snow will fall already the beginning of May I am reflecting upon 1 theater-play that I saw many years ago I am reflecting upon 1 large ∫ : written by hand : it reminds me of 1 thin strand of hair that grew on the nape of my neck .... suddenly I heard, lying on my left side, the chirping of the thermometer which I hadn't heard till then it was like the twittering of birds, giant shine of the morning, from the GRAMO Antony and the Johnsons, <u>I had gone a bit nuts</u> dying hydrangeas, you know, passing by, this year we missed it, how the budding chestnut branches ach how they lay there, sawn off, on the lawn, and us weeping, I mean Max Ernst's "Leaf Customs" so I allowed it : I allowed the landscape to be totally illuminated so that I could see into every angle = ARCADE of my consciousness, namely, <u>searching for the traces of my love-memory</u>, &c., 3 days and nights I FRITTERED away on slips of paper, something hurts, it was blowing, the wind through our hair, what perfume were you wearing in 2010, on May 8, 1945 we crept out of the air-raid bunker <u>and everything was in bloom</u>. I mean the pale birds at the window, if I look for a certain book, it happens that in the course of the search I stumble upon 1 other <u>just-as-longed-for</u> book that I had <u>also</u> been looking for for the longest time, as though it were the true virtue, the state of being chosen "of the body from the orchard" &c. You look more and more like your mother, I say to myself, I dreamed last night of X. and that I pulled him toward me and kissed him and especially that I bit him on the lip which made him cry out .... we strolled then down the deserted NASCHMARKT and discovered again the giant Mediterranean potted plants = plantings = plant-tongues, while Valérie B. upon saying goodbye whispered something, into my ear, IN THE FIRMAMENT OF HEAVEN, that is the mother-brothers called "now take heed once more, you my readers" : St. Augustine XIII, xIx. With the word _slip_ I score my cheek, my arm, my fingernails are torn, I score my arm till it bleeds, don't I .... "*but I'm a witch*," sings Antony, laughed like 1 yg. deer, and then I went to the WC and combed my hair in a falling direction = <u>final departure</u> as though I were 1 waterfall before the mirror etc. Mother lived only for me as she said when Father died, she loved the meerkats in the zoo so we went for a walk in the zoo, *but I'm a witch*, says Antony, he wore his hair in a bob and I listened to the weeping song of Antony Hegarty, this preface-mania, you say, this mania for prefaces which point your sentences in the right direction &c., these flames in the library, I was looking for the Trakl poems (Rosarium), I was looking for the poems of Georg Trakl, I kissed you on the mouth, now it will not snow anymore .... the little lamb namely, <u>in a trice</u>, we were flocking into the cloudages they had flown into, in endless devotion. <u>It was the elite of the whole world</u>,"

6.5.13

"this, this was the ecstasy as I awoke at 4 in the morning, it blew into my room so that I saw everything, blurred, and I cried because I was gripped by the fear that I (would) go blind, Wollschläger's "Herzgewächse" waltzes after the sparkling mountains (so) idyllic cherry blossoms next year, &c., it drove me wild ach the bellflowers it drove me wild that I could hear the bellflowers, tolling, I felt : and now it would not snow anymore, anagrams of the sundown, well I mean, Mama's gentle INNER BREEDING and suchlike. Maybe indeed a bit of FOREST AIR I thought (wished for, and such), well I mean, rapturous feelings when by your side, at times, into the cloudspray, or Café Jelinek where the slow combustion stove glowed, and the YOUTHS with tattoos and piercings etc., and I, hunched over, sipped the coffee grown cold, NEMESIS = global justice, I reverberated, the thunderclaps seemed to clothe themselves : in longing : in purple gladiolas .... for your sake into the bar "ON," something green somewhat-greenish figure, actually gray, in a long gray gown stealing into the corridors of the hospital, stealing in : heavily sedated back then June 2000 after he died : no memory of what I thought or felt or who came to visit, tearless. The bushes in the glass mug : delusional, I say, "flying sheaths of light" .... ardently little caplet adieu : I let myself go to seed, when 1 mirror shatters, there is 1 bad luck, in Schiller Park as we ran through the budding, trees, I bent 1 strand of your hair, when I wear colors the world seems offended, I am now going down the path of my mother, the path of my father, my ex is the gd. God, the Thaya made speed, ravenous, couple of meadows and bushes .... you're 1 Tachist my memory is blank at 5 in the morning. Whereas the cicada the cuckoo, I tore myself from sleep blindly ach he shat so kindly as we were tailoring those afternoons and the turtledoves on the roof, COOED, etc., so exalted this spring! I reverberated

<u>from it</u> perhaps a bit of forest air .... back then they puffed away so much on the upper floor of the hospital that I threw up, while Franz B. sent me the colorized photograph of a lupine glade. From the glowing tip of the mountain someone called my name I saw that the moon had gone behind a gauze of tears (green adornment in your eyes, wasn't it) while the cuckoos in my chest .... well I mean, in a literary discussion with Eva K. (which she recorded) I embarrassed myself, which had the consequence that afterward I put an end to our first-name basis

I adopted his parlance (which dazzled me like 1 starlight, a bit of wolf, in the bushes &c.) new moon phase and a storm, days of rain, my ringleted hair in the bathroom. My mother my goldcrest, for the duration of a daydream, souvenir namely of those summer days spent in the country (drowsing in the arms of nature etc.) .... I mean it depends presumably on this <u>bird-shirt</u> : on this <u>bird-shirt situation</u>, if we will be seriously ATTRACTED to something, what time of day what time of year if the occurrence will brush us with its mighty wings, that is, I wonder if there is 1 connection to that black-shrouded carriage which, on mild summer nights, would come from the direction of the city center headed to the Central Cemetery, moving almost silently &c., and on each side the pale glow of a lantern, so exalted this spring (<u>the Occident</u>). Bit of forest air, bushes in the glass mug, you are 1 symbol, in the photo you always open and close your right eye. <u>I'll tidy myself up, you know, but I also cry much too much</u>"

14.5.13

"very early in the morning to the window, observing the green hill on which something silver glitters, in a trice silver pigeon something silver also in the sky, like : "baroque painting with clouds" silver flood of tears leas of longing in late May the summer somewhere in the distance please let us go there hand in hand, Beloved, let us go there, PATTERING, or like back then when you were still by my side or I was still by your side along the river which was fuming, a bit. Or you mean to do well by me the riven nights I cut a Matisse out of the newspaper and attached it to the wall ach the willow-roselet the dead-nettle, to lie on your chest : 1 Lettrism. You have gone such a distance that you are only 1 shadow I mean "as 1 wildflow'r that one can never find again ...." Gryphius and oleander (then it will be neither day nor night but in the evening there will be light, churning head down in the morning, you look out, musing .... bleeding, bleeding from the heart, am protégée)

lukewarm

while from the GRAMO nights 1 duet &c., that time in Rohrmoos, do you remember how the wind blew COOL in the morning when we opened the windows to the garden to the garden, you know, site of the flowering plant &c., bushes in the glass mug .... I can imagine the sorrow or the souvenir of those summers in the country in the arms of nature reconciling with myself (tearless), the sphincter must have loosened 1 bit, said the doctor, so that the excrement evermore. Fury over the unreconciled elements etc., I make logical fallacies, that is, buried under blossoms even if it's with the green leaf-treasure so that he exults with his eyes. In one of my most recent texts I tried to express what happened to me when I received your letter : I went a little bit nuts I placed your letter in a safe place so that I could find it again, I mean, I hid it, but then I could not remember where, thus is it difficult to find 1 point of reference, and once again I got lost in a dream : 1 circus town, I wake up at a bird's cry, wet camisole, Colette, behind my temples 1 moderate pain, SKYPING and then it wings its way through my mind : 1 new moon phase, and a storm, perhaps I am 1 modernist (for the duration of a daydream &c.) .... ach something comes to me, as I was writing the études the word "<u>branchlet</u>" kept coming to mind it was with me incessantly (28.5), overnight my hair turned curly, I call out like 1 hoot-owl .... the world is full of HARSH, 1 ray of light bores through me, the flaming hearts "le kitsch" the tailor's dog growls at me I mean with the golden sickle cleared the stars, now you have returned, back then in Schönbrunn walking a long time as the sun went down and holding hands, I can still feel the flaming light behind my closed lids, the reddish balls of the peony buds : Verlaine in the vase I held my breath and spoke 1 Ave Maria. The perforated terrain of my memory, Doris P., and the aromatic acanthus leaves from Lentas, here did I wait for you : you, my beloved : my whirred soul .... you won't believe it, but since I've been wearing this Madonna medallion on a gold chain around my neck, I have only hallowed days, indeed in all the arcades of my love-memory I felt : you had, upon your return, the flaming eyes of your mother, which made you alien to me, and you said, I feel so empty .... my perception has become acute : my hearing, my vision, my tactile sensations"

26.5.13

"played footsie with O.R. as we sat with our friends back then, I remember the flower garlands in the parquet floor of the garden in Schönbrunn &c., Elfriede S. called, said she is pining for the parquet-floor flowers in Schönbrunn : large adornments of garlands, with alpine flowers strewn in, which did not really fit in with the Baroque surroundings .... ach I've become 1 bit hallucinatory, razor-thin bird flowerseas Dufy, am protégée am excessive I EFFERVESCED a bit in the armchair while sitting there effervesced it was an epiphany a relief, everything at my feet wet, and immense confession and incessantly. Ach the sesame wings, cuckoos in my chest or garden maquillage in ornamental air &c. As we entered the metropolis in the car we noticed a road sign depicting a car horn with a slash through it .... corncockles stirred at your feet, pressed flower in a little paper sack full of dust and also found the mother-of-pearl buttons, barred my eyes with my hand &c., nights from the GRAMO 1 duet "what is it, my beloved" and we sat on the grounds of the Naschmarkt, on a little wall in the sun, I'm without an INTERLOCUTOR after I stumbled to the window .... these are the ellipses of my language, you know, hugging the pillow, I mean in the recesses and arcades of my love-memory, I mean when I swing in the Schiller Park I have the feeling of doing something FORBIDDEN and I bent over a tiny green chestnut ("will we pull her through?") which was lying on the path, I mean, I let it slip into my coat pocket, it had very delicate spines and 1 dark insect among them, I mean, I pressed it into the palm of my hand, blew on it ("will we pull her through?"), dreamless night and rain in the morning I hear the individual drops fall into the gutter. Under the kitchen cabinet 1 bright red heart-cherry, it moved me I mean stem and blood and next to it 1 sugar cube in the provinces = provence : flooding so that people had to leave their houses, and in the water mass the green grass drowned, nearly bleached, I mean the rolled-up leaves of the fig tree : I mean he stood with an apron <u>tied around his waist</u> in the doorway, LAUGH-ING, the apron filled with fig leaves his gift to me because he had just come back from the island I mean laughing, tanned by the island sun &c., the apron filled with biblical ablutions &c., the apron, shaking his apron and shook the fig leaves onto the kitchen floor but he, laughing, in this scene looking at the kitchen clock locking his arms around me while the red of the heart-cherries in the firmament while in the background Antony and the Johnsons from the GRAMO. While GEO : JD's GEO withstood death (as is said) or like <u>garden maquillage</u> in ornamental air &c. Something comes to me and sitting <u>severely on the bed</u> I feel like Gertrude Stein painted by Pablo Picasso, with bunches of white lilies (lily glade, heart-cherry-red in the firmament &c.) in my arms, with black silk leggings ("love you dearly") <u>skyping</u> and it wings its way through my mind, where you heard the waves tearless where the little lemon trees .... I wish for the destruction of the anecdote .... etc."

3.6.13

Federchen eines Perlhuhns
zwischen den Seiten deines
Briefes : in der Mappe
deiner Haiku

für Bernadette Haller
7. 6. 13

Featherlet of a pearl hen
between the pages of your
letter : in the portfolio
of your haikus

for Bernadette Haller
7.6.13

"something comes to me, as I was working on the études I kept imagining the Ascension of a <u>branchlet</u>, I locked my arms around your soul, I thought I was losing my mind going dissolutely down the path so that the veiled branchlets .... am <u>ill to my core</u> and am flowing toward it : 1 river 1 brook 1 cloud-dam. In "On," Wehrgasse 5th district on hot evenings : we dipped our feet into the damp grass of the garden namely, between the walls of the neighboring buildings, wool scarf, and <u>Simon says</u> "sparrows : house sparrows : hopping little air-balls in the meadow and daisies veiled clouds of June floating in, <u>sacred "in"-bar</u> "On," in the airs Miles Davis namely, peony flowers and jasmine, Genet in the vase, I remember ach the sesame wings, garden maquillage in ornamental air &c., this literature of tears, these fig leaves in the silver bowl, almost desiccated, warm greetings namely, with many knights and black-knight larkspurs, that was aurora ach into the wee hours (nights from the GRAMO heavy from wine or WHINING) ...." it wings its way through my mind, I tried to meet the world with loving-kindness"

12.6.13

Maria Gruber "on the banks"

"the unsayable. My beloved we ramble at our leisure on the banks
of the red butterfly (myriad ants in the firmament grasses by the
water mountains made of air &c.). These tender associations,
Apulias .... head down churning mornings cataracts of tears, I
mean fire and water the wingbeats of the days and years"

19.6.13

"the little Krampus when I stick out my Lilliput tongue before the mirror (the long teats), I flap like 1 bird my pinions in captivity, namely, depravity, ach my circumscribed life, and in the morning I was done-in &c., bleeding : bleeding from the heart : you look : you look out, musing, <u>my love</u>! it's almost like the time I was with that photographer in the Prater : cold November day, he explained to me that <u>1 photo does not necessarily have to be beautiful</u> : it's more about 1 spirituality, about a delirious light that breaks from the clouds &c., (maybe also about this daredevil leap into irrationality), landscape with cow e.g., cow amid bursts of fire e.g., all by Ulrich Tarlatt .... <u>ravenous, the eyne of the flowers</u>. Fire and water or the philosophizing at the typewriter, I conjure up a cushion cover out of scrap paper, for instance, in a trice : the coruscating PROËM .... classically tear-stained or pop : Antony and the Johnsons = blue slit of the heavens, the wingbeat of the days and years. These tender <u>associations : Apulias</u>, natural curls on your forehead &c., in the quiet street in the morning I could hear only the wind, how it blew how it blew and the clattering of horses' hooves that were, perhaps, drawing 1 carriage .... <u>because I had such large wings</u> : with these words I began the phone call, the tiny daisy Ann Cotten handed me upon leaving ach its soul blown out, my sm. yellow POOL in the morning <u>is the moon, but also 1 teardrop</u>, "heartfoot torn, with blue" Bernadette Haller, have you seen the sounding Waterhouse, sm. kneeling watering can in that I went dissolutely down the path that the veiled branchlets, haiku on purple paper : "I apply lipstick, the cool-red one, then I pull the kimono tight at my neck, and stiffen my body." In the window the pale knolls and hills in the west and above them the sweet, swallows, veil-clouds of June, tears in the light of the jasmine &c., I read the clock backwards, upon waking fixing my gaze on a certain point in the domestic chaos .... <u>ach boy with tears</u>, back then in R. as I laid wildflowers on your pillow do you remember .... no one else made me carry a torch like that, these are the ellipses of language, I mean, hugging the pillow. The thought of <u>bouncing asses</u> in Antonin Dvořák, it wings its way through my mind &c. When one goes to the mountains, that is, OZONE, according to Papa, namely the little sack of blackberries, the almost full moon is 1 tear-drop, and everything was <u>silentium</u>, wasn't it. I don't want any changes, I want everything to stay as it is, but that's not how it works, you say, EVERYTHING CHANGES ALWAYS. Well, Anna Akhmatova : 1 black apple seed covered her left eye, and I flinched, &c."

23.6.13

"am far gone am very far gone I talk to the ants in the loo, I've developed backwards, I've read widely into your membrane into your meandering strides, raw pansy, I've gotten so far away from myself, my inner cinema gone dark again, the mistral lacerates me, the apple seed covering my eye .... like a roebuck behind a tree trunk peeking out = Mother after she stopped leaving the house, peeking out from behind the study door, peeking out from behind the study door into the kitchen, who was keeping house there? (for decades it was her domain, etc.), internet-darling a bunch of jasmine upon waking, and insects : islets of order, you know, amid chaos, I say, amid seas of tears, ach, something comes to me : Beethoven's conversation books e.g., Jesus Maria how the birdlets whirred around &c., you abandoned me, I had conflicting FEELINGS, through 1 keyhole I saw the whole world, the long tips of my hair looped under my chin like a headscarf. Am lonely am senescent, pecked-at speck on the asphalt, have become a pigeon (pigeon-grub) I hop around like an elderly pigeon, pecking over the asphalt, am a bachelor-pigeon unsightly elderly bachelor-pigeon, stinking, I lose my feathers my wool my hair I've become a repugnant creature, and over there the grasslands full of tears tender meadows back then a series of hills on the horizon, back then from the window, in the morning, UK rebate, heavy with tears (am behind the times) .... I'm writing you on a piece of paper the color of summer blossoms, sitting in bed in the morning, your most recent letter lost somewhere in the living room : my room-chaos mirrors, perhaps, the chaos of my long life : there was never ORDER in it, just folly, states of anxiety, intuition .... dear nightingale, I believed I was losing my mind, dear aurora, if you could just send me 1 empty sheet of paper with your fingerprint on it, but do it often, said Traudl Bayer, by going dissolutely down the path so that the veiled branchlets. <u>Flaming over it a bit</u>, I say, pear-yellow in Cornwall, my mirror image at the bottom of the empty cup, it's beguiling when asters, bloom, in the garden kitchen, <u>rhapsodizing phlox</u> &c., freely drove often festively with the automobile overland while the branchlets : I mean the breeze blew the branchlets into our hair &c., yesterday I took a walk <u>as we used to take walks</u> around the block, you know, when (it's) 1 warm day (like today), I mean, to write rosehip. Did it finally PLUNK ME DOWN once more to work, a somewhat sickly withered woman I remembered (since the springtime was water under the bridge), that time when we were lying on the bed nestled into each other with the <u>sun shining in</u>, I mean when the notebook is not to hand : the bedsheet totally scratched in all colors / with felt-tip pen / I am even now drawing your stately figure on our pillow, aren't I, you clutched at your heart and said "slumberless, &c., I'm building waterworks." You said that, near my ear, 1 whispering and you dove deep into my eye, namely your eye was 1 blue flower and it wafted so .... since I wanted to keep reading the book, I turned the page, but there weren't any more words, the text stopped mid-sentence, like GLAS by JD"

26.6.13

"namely, *charity*-garden, thus, parakeets. We trudged through the
meadow-yellow, swung on a wooden bridge, and underneath us,
nimble little fish. Didn't dare to reach for your hand, something
like a double rainbow, you were telling me about your childhood
.... leaning against the boscage (in the bushy distance of your
inner life namely, since we were hiking up through the bosquets)
while the contrails scudded across the sky, a bit Cy Twombly :
trembling, dream on paper. I say to Andreas Grunert : I scribble
on the notepad without looking down = poem, for gigantic eyes
since I am fondling the dog-roses, Mother's favorite flower etc.
.... canoodl(ing) like dog-roses I went nuts from happiness, in
the kitchen the blessing of being with child, n'est-ce pas, allegretto!
the little purse found, a dizzy spell I think and so once again, back
to bed. Because I had such wings, flower of the oleander, I am with-
out an INTERLOCUTOR how I stumbled to the window : sesame
wings and garden maquillage in murky air &c., what doesn't come
from the fiery gorge is worth nothing,"

4.7.13

"stray little lamb slung over your shoulder : when you brought back the white jacket (that I had lost on the way). I saw that you had brought back to me the white jacket (that I had lost on the way), I saw the white jacket : white little lamb (slung over your shoulder) that you had rescued and brought back, saw how you walked, at a leisurely pace, bringing back to me the white jacket that I had lost on the way (slung over your left shoulder). As though you had recovered 1 white little lamb that had lost its way, namely, you brought it back to me &c., I saw you walking at a leisurely pace down the street as though you were bringing back to me 1 little lamb that had lost its way .... whereas, the rhubarb's pink tibiae"

for C.F.
6.7.13

"canoodling like dog-roses I went a bit nuts, allegretto, the little purse found, "*let's go to Australia*" (Antony Hegarty), I tie a string around my finger to remember, Beloved. A few months before she died, her afterlife-body was reflected in the deep green folds of a forest that I caught sight of as we sat at the outdoor restaurant : she was sitting across from me, I wasn't paying attention to the conversation she was having with her friends, instead I stared mutely into the forest's flooding afterlife that was spreading out before my eyes : it was her afterlife, but she didn't know it .... Jesus Maria, the polyphonic : golden bird's-egg world, you know, in the early morning of a July day, ach my love for him lasted 6 months, I was besotted like that although there were days on which I felt nothing for him at all and couldn't understand how I had ever gotten worked up about him. Or whatever I was chattering about &c. I love Erich Lessing's voice it reminds me of yours and then I want to see you again on the spot and hold you, Beloved, shall I tell you how today the dark-blue ink gushed across the morning sky and that I was an orphan again &c. Like Rückert awakened : and the cuckoo had already called .... you must have been lonely yesterday because you wrote so many letters. Then a tear rolls down my cheek the minute I hear Erich Lessing's voice, you know, I feel myself in these years to be so much the child I once was, I wonder why, ach in the loge of my feelings &c., well I mean, as for the green cicada in the village of D., which I pressed to my heart in the summers of my childhood, I'm a gambler, I wrote a SOAP on the love poems of William Shakespeare, back then as I walked around on stilts, listened to a SOAP = shallow genre, true, what doesn't come from the fiery gorge is worth nothing, don't you agree, it was the blood of the strawberries that stained my teeth, ach luxuriating in bucolic realms the Augarten maybe : not wanting to do anything at all the whole day, anything at all, just lie in the grass by your side. This roaming-around this my roaming-around = gambling (will the firmament evanesce? are the bellflowers tolling? will the mountains embark on a journey?) Once I spat at the feet of a lady in the little coffeehouse garden : I didn't intend to do it, it just happened, I was embarrassed, well I mean, it was 1 accident, 1 skeleton &c. Am cuckoo "1 Vermeer!" We weep for the other in us .... a very intimate perceptual network, mixed with holograms of memory, lunatic speech particles, torrents of tears. Empathy for the dying daisy, how she, little head hanging down, holds fast to her very last petal : "he loves me, he loves me not" &c."

7.7.13

"that which Braque called "the random (or the fatal?)," I am enraptured must go back and reread Braque's journals in our hair the branchlets in bucolic realms, the sm. black kittens in my dream scattered. The Bohemian asses bounced to Dvořák's music &c., the ecstasy of the elderflowers the scent of the night-violets the sm. plastic pinwheel in the forget-me-not bed, the clematis blossoms (since the spring is water under the bridge, you know), the blue larkspur .... I walk with the botanist's vasculum into Mahler's summer cottage. The morning abducted me into the softest dreams and I cried ("le kitsch"), she was wearing a towel-turban, ach the truth of dreams, the postcard-greetings from all over the world, then someone knocked on the window and I started, my heart startled while I went dissolutely down the path so that veiled branchlets, in the middle of July the still-decorated Christmas tree in the corner of the living room, almost no needles left, in the morning luster of summery airs ach this tousling this being betousled, and toward evening the sm. garden : <u>sm. twig</u> bobbing into my eye also blossoming umbels in the zephyr, you know (I don't think it was my imagination) .... on a little slate the words : "<u>please polish the white shoes with chalk, I'm so lonely</u>"—(because this July is not sufficiently hot, there are no storms : the rose petals fell onto the armchairs they fell without a sound onto the floor, it's long past midnight : you enflamed me my eyes dry and sleepless I search through the trembling lines of Jacques Derrida, this moss and ivy and purplegrass. Behold, the left eye cries more than the right) .... ravenous (presumably) <u>canoodling like dog-roses</u> I went a little bit nuts. Antony, laughs like a DEERLING, what was it again : by trying to hear what Karin was saying in her quietest voice, I noticed that the polka-dot shawl collar she was wearing (with its, so to speak, freckled past) was burrowing into her very marrow. It was rather l accident or apotheosis = glorification and so forth. Forest hurrying ahead, polyphonic golden bird-world, you know, early in the morning, nothing is moving, not a single leaf in the garden the blackbird namely, rising into the summer sky, listened to a SOAP = shallow genre, what doesn't come from the fiery gorge is worth nothing. Snow in the merry month of May, JD writes "I never knew how to tell a story"—in fact she had forget-me-not eyes, and when I walked into the pharmacy she laughed at me : I was welcome, etc. I mean that time when I visited him in the hospital (laden with bags and sacks) the painter Martha Jungwirth came up to me looking commiserative and I told her what had happened .... with your sm. green hat, ach heavenward, my dearest friend, I sleep away my days and nights, and I'm afraid this is the adumbration of my death, and that it also reveals itself in my deepest dreams. And all the rest would come running (12.7). She stood with me in front of the little summer house and pointed into the woods in the direction in which he, whom I was expecting, had hurried ahead (while his message "in the heart of the gloaming" = JD)"

13.7.13

"to beloved sprite = (EvS) the opal snow in mid-July the ecstasy of the elderflowers too bad into the valleys how swift, am boundless as snow the endless splendor, often I spend all day drawing, 50 sheets full. It is perhaps blessed to write "child," I recognize Dufy in the gardens, we lived in the garden in the grove &c., the polyphonic the golden bird's-egg world, you know, early July morning, nights leaning toward the open window : you can't sleep, opal night, ringlet of the opaline night, panicking "I don't have you anymore" .... as the opaline rabbit still hopped around in your garden : now as a constellation in the July sky a beguiling embrace wasn't it, I'm a flaneur in the meadow hollow, speedwell in the side hedges, I mean we haven't seen each other in a long time : you open your arms wide you call out my name "the falling snow," Jesus Maria : the ear's shell, back then when I was working on the études the moon stayed hidden many nights in a row (= new moon of the soul), nothing moved, not a single petal moved. Well I mean, as for the cicada of the dead beloved, he floated as a cicada one summer night through my open window = EJ (until finally he and the birdlets) .... I slept profoundly that morning, I dreamed profoundly : 1 libertine luster (I mean state of emotional turmoil &c.) in that I SAGELY read others like 1 angel = Jacques Derrida, these tender <u>associations : Apulias</u>, feather of a pearl hen between the pages of your letter, your message "in the heart of the gloaming" &c. "What is it my love," I said, the reddening shoots on the bushes : the bouquet <u>am cuckoo</u> ach I thought I was losing my mind, since the veiled branchlets twigs and zephyr <u>opulent snow</u> in my attic room. Thus, parakeets,"

16.7.13

"<u>to the heavenly father</u>. Through the quiet morning we wandered in R., to our left the dusting river, in such moments I feel so much how the happy MOOD flooded through me as I strode : as we strode, as we were happy, back then. "Help, Mistress, you're like 1 kitten namely, and <u>the noble fir</u> came to your mind : violet-wise the evening sky (skylet) .... it was 1 longing = Varnhagen = to finally roll into this place : this rolling-in you know this repeated rolling-in to the place, or how the place, decorated with green owlets, opened up to us I mean how the green-owlet-decorated place kept opening and opening up to us didn't it" "

28.7.13

"ecstasy of the elderflowers, I had an <u>inkling</u> it was Saturday /
Sunday, but it was actually Tuesday, "too bad into the valleys how
swift," thus, parakeets (this little sprite EvS) .... that time when
I ran out, slamming doors, CRYING, after we had had a fight, but
came back forty-five minutes later (still crying), and he took me in
his arms and kissed me, and as penance prayed 3 x to the pink clouds
: sweet indulgence. "dear Elke, I <u>devoured</u> roughbook 028 : you're
sainted!—I'm not sure if I can come to Berlin in Nov. to read with
you since my strength is not what it once was. Your <u>tr.</u> from Russian
were ravishing, I'd love to have a copy, if you could <u>treat me</u> to 1
few pages, etc., I'm leaving for vacation now in Bad Ischl, much
love!" .... I'm clever, Beloved, the asters in the garden sway their
little heads, so delicate like branchlets or ladybugs = playing
dead. Ach the dog-roses : their mellifluous song, &c. 𝄐 I saw
pink hollyhocks on tall stalks, rose-orbs green and blue in
your garden, the wool blanket smelled like cat, etc., such excellency,
in a state of bliss, listened to Forqueray : 1 longing at water's edge.
<u>To crave this e.g. in the woods</u>. Bit of deer &c., now THE TAKING
BACK OF AN HOMAGE ALREADY RENDERED, Beloved
.... when 1 private calamity occurs that makes one feels ashamed,
I mean, when one feels ashamed of this calamity : how should
one <u>announce</u> it to others : one keeps it to oneself and feels
PROFOUNDLY betrayed, doesn't one, the southwest window hung
with white sheets, to BAN the sun, namely in the *charity*-garden the
sun banner hoisted

<u>thus, parakeets</u>. We wandered along summery paths, leaned over a
swaying bridge, I didn't dare touch your hand, I heard your
beloved voice on the <u>dying</u> telephone (cried, &c.)

The pinafore or ascot, well I mean, at the bedside the little ash-rose, n'est-ce pas, <u>the world-soul</u> .... Weststadt lies in the morning sun you know, "it's my nameday," JD, or CONFIDANT, &c., this sudden voraciousness to possess a certain book (= sudden book purchase), then back at home the frenzied reading of the 1st few pages, then the setting-aside of the book : Casanova, the story of my life, etc., breaking out in a sweat, standing in the old town of Antwerp : I want to go to the airport : can't orient myself (spectral springtime), <u>changing shirts multiple times, eye uncovered</u>. I did not follow him into the cafeteria, volatile conversations, you are 1 person full of secrets, I mean, you have 4 or 5 secrets, CF and Lenchen waving goodbye before leaving 🎵 .... Martin Luther said, "whatever you hang your 🎵 heart on, that is your god," I mean, you say, you're longing for a state that existed 2 years ago = Varnhagen = but you don't know what kind of longing that was, namely you were thinking of <u>the noble fir</u>, and then, in fact, you did cry your eyes out ...."

up to 9.8.13

"that even my heart broke on me .... then a wasp <u>SMACKER</u> on my left leg, wave-like these evening cloudlets, they look like Mozart's periwigs from the hotel balcony you know, I'm boundless like snow : the endless splendor, I often draw all day long, 50 sheets full ("too bad into the valleys and swift") Goethe wrote <u>diagonally</u> on 1 sheet of drawing paper. The July morning had such a blueness : as if dipped into a blue pool, but reminded me also with its Roman figures of paintings by Dufy &c., we lived in the garden in the grove, I recognized Dufy in the gardens : this beguiling embrace. Well I mean, in rural settings I could no longer picture my urban habitation : what had happened? In my kitchen, well I mean, the ant caravans the embers of sun the spiderwebs under the cabinets the bit-into bread on the floor, the halo of a rat scurried between stones on the banks of the Traun while a trout was dished up to us, it was late in the evening and the sky glowed like an open fire .... <u>the practice of lust, and suchlike</u>. In scorching heat we arrived in Altaussee and caught sight of the perpetual snow or perpetual ice on the Dachstein mountains in the western sky, ach the poppy-hut, which brought tears to my EYELETS. While the whispering wind from the mountains <u>combed</u> the surface of the Altaussee Lake so that the gentle waves hurried along "<u>to the heavenly father</u>." Now freely festively the sm. pink watering can was jammed between the straps of the green garden apron etc., <u>it looked so blackthorn</u> so rapturous, I mean the stamped-out opening, the pink clamp : <u>behold</u>! (Greetings to Lenchen : of the sweet lark ach I'm crying my eyes out because the whitethorn is withering, cumulus over the summits)"

11.8.13

ich meine wie verwandelte sich
eine Menschengestalt in eine
Hundegestalt?

↓

es glich einer
Illumination, nicht wahr

I mean how did a human figure
transform into the figure
of a dog?

It was like an
illumination, wasn't it

"she, parted her hair in the middle, this, demarcated her body, it, she said, divides me into 2 halves. When they, the two women, sit next to each other, one sees how delicate is the countenance of the one, how rustic the charms of the other, ... such swallow-matters,

"but I don't know where you are perhaps 1 star in your hand, the Traun so transparent, flowing calmly, yesterday there was a full moon it rose over a green mountain, I'm sitting on the balcony and the mountains envelop me, greetings to Lenchen : of the sweet lark which in Max Ernst whirls up and down the rungs of redemption, &c., well I mean, such thought-work : watering the flowers .... ach bit of deer, tongue in stone in that I sagely read the others like 1 angel = Jacques Derrida, lamentation of the bushes, I put my arms around you, even your sm. disturbance (!), Kirchner writes on 4.8.19 "just work, work and don't think about anything else; paints very fresh; and always give everything beautiful that you have gladly, like a child, etc." I have watered the flowers. 1 sensation a recollection an invention : back then in Athens, on the coast, me wearing a trench coat, crazed with love, following X. with my eyes, who, paying me no mind, was playing ball with our other friends, discussing, considering the sky .... Fluff and nonsense of the heavens, sniveling a bit over it, I say, protegée, how I dreamed the elliptical sentences, will there be kisses from Mama, etc. ach restless pleasure of steps in the night : maquillage and flowers, something mocked me mercilessly. Such a transport : I'm not someone who can speak extempore, in the evening glow her face looked unfamiliar, on the last night in Bad Aussee in the light-blue sky a very sm. white cloud like Mozart's periwig (soundless), these tender associations : Apulias, feather of a pearl hen between the pages of your letter .... what is it, my beloved, the reddening shoots on the bushes or bouquets of May &c., am cuckoo (truth of mourning), but then, when DECAY STEALS OVER ME. That time in R. when I placed the wildflowers on your pillow : although : I never carried a torch like that for anyone else. You asked me, which side is your chocolate side, in this morning's sky the dark-blue ink gushing, yesterday spent the whole day buried in pillows, you must have been lonely because you wrote so many letters, my love, shall I tell you how the dark-blue ink gushed across the morning sky today &c., and that I'm once more an orphan and secretly ("like Rückert awakened : the cuckoo had already called"), the ecstasy of the elderflowers the scent of night-violets the sm. plastic pinwheel spinning in the forget-me-not bed, the larkspur. The morning abducted me into the softest dreams, so soft that in the dreams I was crying. Dreamt last night of Otto B. (with drinking cup), gullet of the privet, bitter, snow, fields of sunflowers facing me, 4–5 x switching out of the communion wafer, &c."

15.8.13

"I never knew how to tell a story, said Jacques Derrida, all our phantasms as I stood on the terrace, the moon seemed to glide into my open arms oh ghost-scenes, the white flowers you carried to me, ecstasy of the elderflowers, scent of the night-violets the sm. plastic pinwheel spinning in the forget-me-not bed, clematis blossoms, larkspur, the morning abducted me into the softest dreams, so soft that in the dreams I was crying .... greetings to Lenchen of the sweet lark, nothing is moving not a single leaf is moving in the park, listened to a SOAP = shallow genre &c., it was the blood of the strawberries that stained my tongue or was it the blood of my heart ach luxuriating in bucolic realms maybe the Augarten : not wanting to do anything, Beloved, not wanting to do anything all day long except lie in the grass by your side, I stood in the Jupiter sun, read 1 poem by e.e. cummings, have a sm. infection, a ganglion on my right hand, I'm irritable in the negative zones &c., I write to Bastian S. "I can't find your enchanting letter, I would have loved to read it again : the Olympia letter. I wondered if in choosing your Christian name your parents wanted to communicate their love of Mozart : at any rate a rare name, which ENNOBLED (?) their very common last name, the circling of our thoughts during our encounter that high summer afternoon at the café seemed to have reached a peak when, instead of the name Gert F. Jonke = one of the first winners of the Bachmann prize, the name of the great Reinhard Priessnitz occurred to me : an imbrication of poetic time-strata? (actually this is the facetious transcript of some early morning emotions immediately after waking—yes, still lying in bed—, in the hopes that you are faring well ....)" .... then a wasp smacker in my left leg, spotted the little wave-shaped white evening clouds, you know, like Mozart's periwig, I heard your voice but you were not there. I mean, I won't be able to forget that sight for a long time

: we were in Altaussee in scorching heat sitting on the veranda of the old inn dazzled by the ice and snow on the Dachstein mountains vis-à-vis, namely, but in this likeness not a single detail will be missing : "not 1 candle-glow not 1 savor not one devotion, do you remember, the eternal ice held by our scorching gazes (28.8)" like the canary at the bottom of the glass, n'est-ce pas. You're crazy, he said to me back then, you're crazy .... what was it with the Olympia letter, I say, was it not that I stood, stood there, next to you, shifting from one foot to the other as you talked with our friends, in the mountains, but I had gotten tired, we were standing in the high meadow which had grown up to our hips, I thought I would break down and it would never end, my feet sunken into the ground etc. In the morning you often asked, "Do we have 1 reading today?" and I always said no, I felt my discipleship keenly, I sat at the breakfast table and thought, "I cannot save the world" .... the flowerlets the deflowering the flowery language, I couldn't comprehend it, how the yellow bellflowers grew back every night after every evening they were mowed down, they simply sprang back up through the loamy soil, yes, I waited every morning full of longing to see them in the fire of the morning sun, I mean "I am 1 liberal aesthete" : see JD "Glas," p. 242, in my gardenlet. Well I mean, I'm wasting away with longing for you, the eternal ice on the shady side of the Dachstein mountains dazzled my eyes, the redundancy of sunsets, with grace,"

up to 28.8.13

"as we sat on the veranda of the old inn in Altaussee, ach how the eternal ice, held by our scorching gazes : how dazzled our eyes were, weren't they, how still, ach broken heart, this was "for the visualization of a glacier (seen from Altaussee, this sweet work of a mountain range : shady side of the Dachstein mountains, e.g.,)" de mon urine, Georges Bataille, too bad into the valleys how swift, I'm clever, Beloved, the asters in the garden with their headlets wafting. It was all very edifying, you say, the gladiolas in the tall grass &c., I picked a red gladiola to think of Jean Genet, whose body resembled a red gladiola .... an idea pops up, already forgotten. Out of the dust, out of the trash, you say, out of the most profound filth alights the intoxication of the most glowing blossoms : the shepherd's purse the Turk's cap lily the gladiolas, of Jean Genet, to the heavenly father .... thus, parakeets, the ecstasy of the elderflowers, Beloved, shall I tell you how the dark-blue ink gushed out across the morning sky, &c., how I am once more an orphan and covertly, nothing can be imagined without its opposite. Your Olympia letter and I cried so as though it were raining on a summer morning, and I wandered e.g. around my block and the like, today the dark-blue ink gushed out over the morning sky, sweet deliverance, as penance prayed to the pink clouds, I put on Purcell's "Fairy Queen," gullet of the privet bitter, snow, ach do you remember, those prized overland drives where we roared along through the lush woods, the flowerlets the deflowering the flowery language, she could not comprehend how the yellow bellflowers could grow back overnight I mean they sprang back up through the soil at night, yes, she waited for it in the morning, for the flowers in the fire of the morning sun, before the gardeners began mowing the tall meadow before her window etc., whereas the park-goers had nodded off on their benches, a teardrop on the living-room wall, well I mean, still, vanities. End of August. It is late morning, nothing can spur me on. Someone, I don't know who sent it, wrote me a note : "<u>Persevere</u>" .... pinchbeck, I am wasteful like the talents of the mother of my mother whom I loved very much : she lifted me, February 1927, onto a bench in the Rubenspark and held my sm. hand : I forget who photographed this scene etc., I freeze even in summer, I did not want to accept that Jacques Derrida's GLAS was ending—what was I supposed to read now, I would start again from the beginning, high-feverish color-cosmos, under the ash tree .... in the dream I perceived fragrances : synthetic fragrances, the fragrance of my favorite perfume 1 flower = 1 gauze in my left eye, 1 pinchbeck, hunched over with smushed breasts in the foxhole. Back then <u>in a bathing costume</u> on the Cobenzl whole days spent in the water ("how one tests the water with one's toe") <u>and Father snapped photos</u> : I'm stretching toward an imaginary ball, he wanted to record my figure, was presumably proud of me. Well I mean, we WANDER down the allées in the Burggarten it is wonderful we hold each other's hands (for how many summers now), as the delicate yield of a tree in an early autumn breeze blows away, so my once VALIANT hair blows away / scatters in all directions, these snaking threads : how repellent, I read a bit in Seamus Heaney, I say, I mean back then, that weekend in Spain, when he bought me a fan because it was so hot, so still. This secret drawer in the conference room at school to which I also had a key etc. I stuffed it full of love-offerings for him, which annoyed him"

up to 5.9.13

"Madonna! my soul hissed out of my body. The half-moon rode over the grand hall of the mountains. While we were in Altaussee sitting on the terrace of the inn, contemplating the eternal ice across the way, for my bloodbath, we mother each other, writes Roland Barthes, when we kissed in the physics lab my left arm got in the way .... I started to cry because I felt that I had been treated unfairly, and when I looked at my face in my pocket mirror I found that I did in fact look quite pitiable. I gave some love-offerings made of plastic to a dear friend who returned them to me immediately which was devastating and suchlike, my perception had become acute : my hearing my vision my tactile sensations .... ach mignonettes, long after midnight : moss and ivy and purplegrass my left eye weeps more than my right, very intellectual, you say, off-the-rails voice I mean lyrebird .... one day I will have to leave all of it behind, will have to leave everything, my old Christmas tree, my books with the bookmarks placed inside them, the little dog with the heavenly gait &c. I'm allowed only

[natural] food says the doctor, I have long been sitting between heaven and earth, and I cried so as though it were raining on a summer morning, Antony on the GRAMO, you know, when you don't praise my writing lavishly I'm instantly discouraged .... of a foxlet or serrated bird, namely to make AMOUR, we make AMOUR while the cloud-fluff in the morning, the cloud-gauze in the evening = in my gardenlet. Well I mean, I'm wasting away for you (bit of a disheveled shirt and ossicles so I hang around cry my eyes out and search for words that, into the abyss ....) I mean that fall into the abyss, and I stare a long time

at the photograph of him with a sm. pipe, defenseless, <u>where has he voyaged to</u> = <u>like the God particle</u>. The veiled branchlets, then a teardrop rolls down my face I am listening to the photographer Erich Lessing on the radio, I hear Erich Lessing's voice it reminds me so much of yours that I wish <u>to see you again on the spot</u>. Am cuckoo : 1 Vermeer!, we weep over the other in us, this blowzy state sm. twig bobbing into my eye (in that I went dissolutely down the path) also blossom-umbels = wisteria clusters = in the heavenly breeze &c., I mean stem and blood next to it, <u>1 sugar cube in the provinces</u>. Am haunted by such visions : I was standing with the little cherry-basket on my arm in the courtyard of the building at Prinz-Eugen-Strasse 18 as she, entering the courtyard / whose life was full of cherry-blood, I mean, I wanted to greet her by holding out my hand but she refused me hers : in another dream I was melancholy : 1 civil servant was speaking to me in a government office but I could not understand him : he wore a fancy felt hat and looked like Minerva, <u>in part I always provoked the same phrases, didn't I</u>"

7.9.13

"such big raindrops (<u>yesterday after canoeing</u>) today blustery wind and be you hailed and blessed, "in bright dreams have I often looked upon you" after Alfred Gold, 1893, by Arnold Schönberg, I want to implore my language hither &c., the lambkins namely, in a trice, we flocked into the cloudages they had flown into, in endless devotion, my heart deeply distressed I mean the 1st tears-day, it is raining in my heart you know my 1st tears-day because you flew away : your absence in the fire, I will pass the time of your absence in cafés. Botticelli painted the baby Jesus with the crown of thorns on his wrist as if it were a toy, I want to escape my fate, these ECHOS in my language n'est-ce pas, when will the wound close

from my father I inherited <u>this need for rapture</u> ....
your handwriting tells me that you are reliable (read off a note from Andrea N.) &c., I freeze even in summer : the swallow-shrieks .... <u>you spread the holy moths</u> from my abode to yours, "la passione" of Haydn = unfailingly unloved (could yield a nice book title?), for each date a drop of blood, JD, the yg. Japanese woman spoke to me on the street, "where do you live now?" = I had lived on that street in my childhood and early youth = she was wearing huge sunglasses so I couldn't see her eyes, and I answered her question. Thus do I more and more resemble my mother, during a walk in the sun with Mother hand in hand : during a slow walk in the sun <u>that time, namely, the sparrows</u> : how they flitted about in the already almost leafless BUSH : flitted and haunted me who could not stop crying helplessly crying while the church bells (namely, quasi-rosary &c.), bit of dung on the duvet : I don't dare go to the WC and miss your <u>cherrying</u> phone call : <u>cherished</u> phone call ....
Objects slip from my hands, went walking in the Spreewald with Michael Hamburger, Hebbel as poet a bit WOODEN, the firelight,

the firelight in the armpit, he WAS 1 BLOGGER. I thought in my soul I was awakened, the cuckoo had called. I've been stone-deaf for ages, said Mother one morning upon waking .... special pen writes upward when I'm lying down e.g. <u>I want to flood my language hither or along</u>, underneath the kitchen cabinet a well-formed red heart-cherry I mean stem and blood, and next to it 1 sugar cube IN THE PROVINCES &c., I find 2 leaflets of blood-red bougainvillea from last summer (my heart-blood I gave you to drink .... "le kitsch" &c.), back then the budding chestnut forest, Otto Sander dead. How am I supposed to bear your absence it tears my heart out, <u>so I let myself go to seed</u> .... I also found 1 blood-red bougainvillea leaflet, it is 1 bit crinkled, from your last stay on the island. My tears do in fact taste salty like the sea at its shores. I mean you simply departed without saying goodbye, I will cross off each day drawing to its close on my pocket calendar until you return, the sun is a communion wafer, maybe, that I will let dissolve on my tongue I will swallow it so that it can never rise again, &c., of a foxlet or bird you know, that which Braque called THE FATAL .... these are the ellipses of language <u>I mean hugging the pillow</u>, and always a bit of a lie you know. Rain in the morning, and I listen to the drops knocking in the gutter"

up to 16.9.13

"ach little Xmas tree, little kosher Xmas tree, spat : start, starting to rot these bones in the banged-up moon, I brood in the mornings says Elisabeth von Samsonow, in the little shopping bag Blanchot's SADE and 1 red-cheeked apple. You call me on the telephone and I don't hear the ring : you are terribly far away : I burst into tears. To have missed your call is tantamount to betrayal .... already cold this fall morning, ach my little Xmas tree the heavens are rampaging the sun smokes 1 kitten made of pink tin-foil on the wooden floor, back then the hammock in the garden, souls of the vetch of the night violets and dahlias dragonflies and rainbows, I was 8 I didn't know what 1 paradise it was &c., the days were 1 day, I sat on the fountain steps, the horizons 1 violet rivulet, with bare feet in the dust of the village road .... you are my 1st thought in the morning you are my last thought at night, we cried together, Beloved, Dante points with a brown hand to an open book in which he has written, this passion of a poesy, as if one had been separated from one's beloved without 1 word of goodbye without waving without blowing kisses whereas 1 host of wildflowers etc., namely as one tests the water with one's toe, best wishes and pansies, from Paris, I'm steering toward sweet letters .... Lambkin's cake, the lamb's head butchered, under the blue tatterlets of the heavens (in the caves of the body), starting to cry at those tatterlets, sepia-colored the birds with stiffened little hands gripping the branchlets of spring, withered gnarled little hands = <u>violet-arthritis</u>, n'est-ce pas, sputum-like cellophane on the linoleum floor where sugarloafs, lashed heart, where claw : the little songbird's claw contorts, and twittering as arias its throat exudes, boughs in heaven = early spring's grief, n'est-ce pas .... to remember V's name, I say, I must picture my handwriting in the top-left corner of a fig leaf : days of supplication when you are not there, I say, misty eye supplicating, already the 2nd tears-day, 3rd rain-day, you know, I go barefoot out of the house. I opened my eyes. In my left pants pocket there was an empty Swed. nutshell, I held my cheeks and I said so much happened while you were away but I don't remember, a green landscape under my feet while Michael Heltau said, I believe you are an evening beauty, or how one tests the water with one's toe. "Fevering the litany-flower you know (with Uli R., whose birthday is today, occurred the repetition of a sensation in a train station in Munich, namely she was confused by the observation that I was able to perceive the fragrance of a <u>thundering</u> bouquet of lilies, which, as it appeared, confounded her very much, which is to say, she did not wish to presume that in my great = <u>thundering</u> age, I would be able to perceive the mysterious = <u>thundering</u> fragrance of the lilies : which very much wounded me once more, etc.)," and I saw <u>the magnificent moon</u> riding over the mountains"

up to 30.9.13

"to the heavenly father to Enrico ....

        the little ring I once gave to you and
        that you returned to me : now it lies in
        my room (ach) in dust ....

fleur in my garret, I mean in the morning these big bouquets of
gladiolas in yellow magenta and pink like Arabella's state of sleep
("yelling eventually," JD) I mean the calendar's refrains I
mean those extreme phone conversations that my throat, that throt-
tled my throat. I always had to cover <u>my</u> head so the colony of bats
wouldn't harm <u>me</u> etc. The people from TV asked me to sit down
at my typewriter and simulate the stroke of genius, which, however,
I declined to do .... l'amour &c. Maternal grandmother, this love-
liest fairy of my early childhood who accomplished everything with
one hand I recollect the most magical blossoms in her décolleté,
dried fig leaves still in the glass mug, whereas l host of wildflowers
.... <u>you're my adagio</u> and pink hollyhocks bloom on your cheeks,
and sweet swift sparrows CRAZED WITH LOVE carried you
across the black earth. He said "I brood in the morning I brood in
the evening," you are my 1st thought in the morning you are my
last thought at night .... I shout at things when they slip from my
hands : I scold things when they slip from my mouth. Ach where
are you my little Xmas tree, the sun fumes the heavens rampage,
my grief great at having missed you, little Xmas tree ach little
kosher Xmas tree the happiest bosom of God when you came &c.
I mean I was standing with him (on a cool spring morning) on a
swaying wooden bridge and I felt the urge to brush his hand, which
was holding fast to the railing, but it didn't happen, <u>it began</u> to rain

l spell of the finest rain so we walked off the bridge and <u>he began</u> to tell me about his childhood ....

(I have developed ticks, &c.)"

15.10.13

after Stefan Fabi's cardboard collage "Naked" (2013) and woodcut "Man with Flute" (2013)

"he grabbed me under my arms and lifted me up : then he bedded me down on the sofa and slipped in under the covers and I was his flower that he carefully crushed, while the night made of reeds, felt, and bones and so we lay there the whole night not moving, it was the night that was EVERLASTING the stars were falling but we did not move, nobody can understand, a night made of bones, reeds, and felt. "Shall we sleep 1 little bit now" he said as the morning opened its eyes, and we slept holding each other (and nothing happened), that is to say, we went into the 3rd dimension which everlasting ....   I hug and greet you :
chamber-flutters

        (as the morning opened its eyes he began to play his pan flute which was made of bones felt or reeds &c., while the wilderness of the sounds)

(kept his hood on / I drink water from my cupped hand, red poppies 1 sm. bird skull on our bed ....)

        ("here again I do nothing else, I can do nothing else but quote, as you perhaps just saw : I have discovered many new words, and yet for want of others I keep coming back to the same ones")
        JD"

22.10.13

126

"I'm feathered, can shake paws, am mourning the sweet word ZWITSCHERN, I can hardly bring it across my lips anymore because behind it lurks the word TWITTER what happened? what happened to our beautiful German bird-language .... the rolled-up wilted yellow scrolls of the daffodils &c., while the eagle's train back then in those summers in R. over our heads I mean how Arnulf Rainer painted them, as we glided along the forest paths strewn with spruce needles : glided along as the train of the eagle of Arnulf Rainer as we in the pixie woods back then in R. as he handed me a crushed wildflower as we chased through needles and leaves, in verses, I am very innocent in the meadowland, I found a little walking-stick in the meadowland, I'm wasting away, still crying in the meadowland, aren't I, still crying back to bed as the scenery in Francis Ponge .... when I woke up this morning both swans were already circling over the lake and their wingbeats touched my cheeks wet with tears. Ach the dreams had disappeared they were biblical dreams with white feathers and pure voices that made me blissfully happy, and I sank down with the words "hurry to help me" into the meadowland, because you called me early in the morning you cleaved through my deep sleep, Klaus Reichert whispered to me recommending "Nuages gris" by Franz Liszt, freely drove often festively with the automobile overland while the branchlets I mean the gentle breeze blew the branchlets into our hair &c., yesterday (I) took a walk as we used to take walks around the block when it was a warm day, you know, rhapsodizing phlox (end of October) .... back then, namely, as we walked through the dark-green forest, that is to say, as I hiked with my parents on the Cobenzl, that must have been in another lifetime. Pan flute of fate that the dew on my forehead dripped into my eye, while the wilderness of the stars while crying to the tatterlets of the heavens, yellow like the canary on the bottom of the glass, n'est-ce pas / you are crazy he said to me you are crazy, you are ambivalent he said. 1 halo over the mountain : 1 silvery cloud .... I have a little bit of cancer, she said, but her appearance was rosy, I rifle through these quivering lines, ach mignonettes, long after midnight mosses and ivy and purplegrass. As we made AMOUR as we hoisted the cloud-fluff in the morning, listened to Erik Satie on the GRAMO in the morning in the evening : Three Pieces in the Shape of a Pear (etc.) .... how miserable am I they treat me like 1 child, dreamed I was 1 bird flapping my wings, dreamed I was 1 razor-thin bird 1 gold-finch, for example, shedding a tear, a bluetit, for example, my wings like ice crystals, you know .... I'm mouthless (she said "pi-pi," I construct mnemonic devices I barred my face, Confra. The 1st half of the year had flown off, was done in, like flags in wind) I live in symbiosis with violet bushes, I (still) have 1 lantern or love affair, this sequence with the cloth-of-gold, at bottom, I have wasted my life. He accompanied me across the street it was 1 icy winter day he wasn't wearing a coat, not just what is written, but existence, too, must be poetic"

up to 31.10.13

"as we traveled across America '71 Ely wanted to see the Grand
Canyons <u>at any cost</u> but I was a bit afraid of such an undertaking
.... in Bloomington we visited a friend who greeted us with a
bouquet, I mean, of wild damp tuberoses, and see, pink clouds
glowed in her dream-language. A large body of water lapped at my
feet while pansies = pensées of noon, and he said "we're all so
attached to you it's unbelievable" .... indeed. Where on the lane
the moon <u>shimmered</u>, &c."

5.11.13

"well in general I was waiting for someone to dictate to me the following text: I have 1 sm. stove in my kitchen upon which coffee steams or fumes from a sm. machine &c. Where on the lane the moon shimmers "after he had crept quietly on WOLF-SOLES to the altar .... namely shoved aside the double curtains in the hotel room and then swallowed 1 dainty communion wafer (JD)"—here cunt and maquillage and crowns of flowers : 14 ½ years ago we planted a rosebush on his = Ely's grave : there were almost 500 mourners at his funeral, they all passed before me to kiss my hand or cheek I stood for many hours at the open grave till I started trembling = SHAKING : till my doctor, who was standing behind me, said to me, that's enough. So we left him, and over us floated a dove, like a cut-off piece of fruit &c., to the heavenly father (Maria) also with *WAX*, sealed the letter with wax with a red seal, that is, the garden-like, music from the dance-cabinet, you know, in the photograph your eyes full of longing, thorn-plays (Jean Paul), you are infinite you are inflamed, e.g. into the Wiesental valley. 1 day after tomorrow, time is dissipating quickly. Dreamless night and rain in the morning that knocked at the window, objects fall from my hands, rampaging wind yesterday after canoeing (all hail) .... the sun is a communion wafer and I let it dissolve on my tongue : I will swallow it so that it will never rise again, and then the world will be dark like my soul, and die. Oh my little Xmas tree : kosher Xmas tree, you borrowed my bright child's umbrella, I will duck down behind the violet mountains so no one will ever be able to find me (purges like 1 fart, &c.) ach horizons, lashed, horizons. As we traveled across America '71, Ely wanted to see the Grand Canyons at any cost but I was afraid of such an undertaking. In Bloomington we visited a friend who greeted us with a bouquet, I mean, of wild damp tuberoses, and see, pink clouds glowed in her dream-language.

A large body of water lapped at my feet while pansies = pensées of noon, exactly. Where on the lane the moon shimmered, &c. Ach Beloved a cous-cous (kiss-kiss) for you also I found 1 red bougain-villea petal from your time on the island and a Cretan stone that almost broke my heart, as a child I liked to read the fairy tale about the ruby .... it seemed to me that he had come to interview me he wanted to interview me he stood at the door with a little basket and smiled &c. as though he were expecting something beautiful, for example, the train of flowers, n'est-ce pas ("fire take this wood, fire"), they treat me like a child, I said to the doctor, I saw the Sacred Heart again on the display, 1 razor-thin bird in the pine woods, undaunted the buds in the park we are sitting in the Rüdigerhof, ach mignonettes long past midnight, today you will not visit me through the tall grasses I look deep into your flower-eyes, you walked in, a white scarf slung around your neck also snakes and swallows, Anglo-Saxon inundation of our German language, your soul full of cherry-blood &c. Kurt N. says, your writings are echoic inventions ...."

up to 7.11.13

"Nursery rhyme from the '30s : It's raining drip drop it's raining and won't stop the flower-petals are wet and the butterflies are headed to bed. Red red butterfly come oh do not hide, but your little brother must stay outside ....

where on the lane the moon shone and snow shimmered, a communion of snow and disheveled birdlet &c., you are my 1st thought in the morning you are my last thought at night, and then I dream about you, where on the lane the moon shines as this language fraternizes with my aching raving delirium doesn't it. Maybe my earliest memory she set me on the kitchen table which was covered in a red = white polka-dot oilcloth and washed me (we had no bathtub), it was the same table on which she washed the raw vegetables .... I saw, near Flanders, that the lilac bush next to the telephone booth had been cut back, feather in my hair 1 pigeon had flown overhead .... ach I'm slipping away into the beyond I am a marsh-marigold am already halfway in the earth, death is 1 nuisance : 1 withered rolled-up leaf on the kitchen table &c., I have a car full of drums infinite feverish totally daubed, the sundown. This sequence with the cloth-of-gold, I say, would have made 1 nice beginning, this flower presumably had something to do with John Cage, I say, that time he accompanied me across the Hauptstrasse it was 1 icy winter day but he wasn't wearing a coat, instead of drumming with fingers, I have wasted my life, I live in symbiosis with violet bushes, I still have a LANTERN, or love affair everything at a standstill : larches in the garden, pine trees and cypresses. There was something with cherries but I didn't note it down (he stood at the door with a little basket of cherries on his arm and wanted to interview me) .... Confra. The 1st half of the year had flown by I mean it was done in, like flags in the wind, we went for a walk, 1 inkling of cherries, naked. <u>In a stomach pit</u>. 1 little allée dog, quiet November day, I let myself go to seed—back then with Ely, I say, we talked about the summer and that this time we weren't going to spend it in the mountains, ADIEU. These art genres in honey namely, <u>please let's go to the Stadtpark</u> : JASMINE. He followed me (even) to the bathroom and called out, now we can finally invite <u>our darling</u> to dinner, can't we, I have become mouthless, ach these never-ending nights where on the lane the moon shone where on the lane the moon shimmered where on the island the writing of the waves, the redundancy of sunsets (with grace), in the morning we listened to Erik Satie's Three Pieces in the Shape of a Pear, "don't be so boundless …….. " "

14.11.13

"fevering, the Chinese lantern plant (the ferret) ach the force of fate glowing throat of the amaryllis, on stilts : the clipped cloistered stem of the amaryllis in the glass, green-locked bud tilting into the beyond, repetition of a sensation : scent of a <u>thundering</u> bouquet of lilies, graceful shadow of a woods .... what befell me, I say, when something befalls me, I say, there's something evil in the air, I say (will e.g. the wall fall down and strike me dead?) .... "*wool* is *cool*" : in my great <u>thundering</u> age, I found myself in a slumbering state, laughing Mother's prosthesis on the farm table, I hardly think in sentences anymore, opened the letters with my thumb (we sallied forth through the green woods e.g. into the Wiesental valley, "how green the woods, that I strode through" Theodor Storm, my mirror image on the bottom of the half-empty glass : miniaturized). This razor-thin bird, I say, my bedsheet covered in scrawls, I say, with felt-tip pen, even now I am drawing your figure on the pillow, I look feverishly for Francis Ponge's "Notebook from the Pine Forest," namely on wolf's feet in the morning, she opens her apartment door and says, I heard you tripping up the stairs, billy-goat gruff, n'est-ce pas, the long Passion, I bar my face with my hands, my stilt-walking at midnight, I say, this sweet work of a mountain range = for the visualization of a glacier, seen from Altaussee, I am multimorbid &c., "can't you AT LEAST <u>produce 1 bit of stool</u>" says my doctor, spiderwebs between the casemates in my kitchen, I say, but then she died soon afterward. The moon came riding over the mountains, it was an ecstasy, you know, it was a devotion. She sat down opposite me and said it was all just platonic, it was 1 milky morning, I was stunned = read off a note from Andrea Niessner, ach denuded FULGURATION in the Spreewald, your hopelessly with open arms, your world-fire : cherry-blood. I mean where <u>the pixies</u> back then in Rohrmoos ("le kitsch" &c.), he gave me a wilted woodland-flower, we ran through the forest along the paths strewn with spruce needles—o! we glided down (butterfly's train), I'm feathered can shake paws, your Olympia letter! and in the underground parking garage yesterday 1 incandescent pigeon, she will come to you she will come to visit you, you know. Do you remember the afternoons on the Cobenzl we spent with green branches the earth roaring, then came Ajax the messenger with elegiac strophes .... ach my rebellious *dasein*, and suddenly I think of the name GESSWEIN = the school director under whose aegis = morion I had for years &c. Then I cried in the inn garden in which the sparrows sprang around (lustfully) in the HIGH GREENERY, I mean, I cried while the sparrows hopped around in the gloomy greenery, the gloaming &c. I enjoy using the word spoon which can also mean rabbit's ear : I invoke the word for the shape of your ears when you sleep on them, one sleeps on one's ears till they go deaf and numb, my right ear when I sleep on it feels numb, I remember she was standing at the splenetic bus stop, when you sleep on your right ear, I say, bells ring .... bit of deer &c., GLAS by JD means death knell. It was in Bad Ischl and we were eating I think sausages, in the corner of the living room, my time is dying down &c. When in God's name I (sit) on the toilet my focus dissolves : my knees appear to me as the two hemispheres of a vanishing (of an early spring). My two ears folded up like the spoons of a rabbit that is sleeping. How she stood there in her senseless chemise, before I thought I noticed the beginnings of a rounded back, which alarmed me, this state of emotional turmoil : leaf-trilling"

17.11.13

Westwind bläst aus vollen Backen

West wind blows out of full cheeks

"my melancholy muse, I had written 1 †, butterflies and folds affixed with a sewing needle, which was 1 oracle, working with him was 1 walk in the park, said the psychotherapist. We haven't seen each other in a long time .... to me it was as though when we reached the church square that night in Neubeuern I mean the sm. houses congregated <u>in a pilgrimage</u> around you, I loved you more than anything in the world, as we (bivouacked) those 2 days in the cold room in Neubeuern and you, the stove, I mean how you BLEW UPON the stove. "Fire take this wood, fire," in the eye-blink of awakening I saw 1 bed of irises, I was looking for a certain book and into my hands fell "The Violence of the Real" on Francis Bacon, I was beguiled, as I walked into the kitchen I could smell a botanical green I saw the vase with the <u>collar</u> = *Kragen* of flowers (standing) on the floor. It sounded like 1 little bell ringing when the felt-tip pen rolled off the table : onto the bottle which was on the floor next to my bed &c. The rampaging : the SPARROWS in that bush <u>or hedge</u> by which we sat late in the evening talking : 1 sort of discourse perhaps or crisis back then in Bad Ischl, and how they rampaged! : SPARROWS! : hopping around! in that bush or hedge upon whose shoulder we were leaning .... as I turned around 1 x while hiking up the path to the terrace to consider the distance I had come, I looked one MOMENT long into a blossom just opening (in a field) below me, thanks to much crying my mind had been washed clean, as we entered the concert hall to listen to 1 concert of a SERIES, I stayed behind Ely who was trying to forge a path through the thronging crowd while I felt the gazes of the spectators coming to rest on me I reached for his hand which he had held out behind him like 1 dry leaf, back then I was 1 bit proud and as the music started I laid my hand on his, the prologue of our love had begun, thanks to much crying my face had been washed clean .... agitated dreams and frolicked over the deserted Nasch-markt. Well I mean, it bills and coos, the dawn (you are my whole happiness), le kitsch, &c. as if I were once more striking through everything that had already been depicted, the yellow rolled-up scrolls of the daffodils, oh my little Xmas tree!, Klaus R. recom-mends to me Franz Liszt's late work "Nuages gris" for piano, Kurt N. says, your writings are echoic inventions, that was in the summer, but now it is winter. My porous morning sleep through which the voice of the newscaster drummed in droplets, I say, but I couldn't catch the content perhaps parapluie or parade, where-upon the rain in droplets drummed, Ely's white curls among my typewriter keys .... that you telephoned : did I dream it or was it 1 hallucination did I visit Carlfriedrich Claus back then in the GDR or did I dream it ("stay lying there, angel, till I return," Thomas Kling), then dusted the dust bunnies in the corner of the room, out-side the fog-clouds THE SOUSE &c., that which reveals itself and that which conceals itself, as you wrote that time, handwrote letters in the air and I had to guess the word, ach Mr. Treppschuh, we laughed so hard .... the summer-saint in the midst of winter"

up to 29.11.13

"on the wall the shadow of my beloved mother, stenography in the cahier. The ecstasy of the elderflowers, thus, parakeets, too bad into the valleys how / swift. That time when I ran off after slamming the door, crying after we had argued, but came back a few hours later still in tears, doorknocking, and he took me in his arms and kissed me .... as sweet indulgence prayed to the pink clouds, ach the branchlets' mellifluous singing. The asters in the garden wafting their headlets (All Souls' Day) wool blanket smelled like sick cat, you know, southwest window hung with white sheets, to ban the sun, through the Jewish cemetery like a primeval forest as we slowly drove : 1 whirring of gray birds the staging of wolfish shrieks .... train of little thunderflowers back then in Rohrmoos where the pixies he gave me 1 meadowflower, we hurried through the woods down the paths strewn with smooth spruce needles ach we glided along : we glided along into it, when I in GOD'S NAME in the WC. Dissolving my focus. My knees appeared to me as a vanishing, &c., my two ears folded like the ear-spoons of a rabbit that is sleeping, Botticelli painted the Christ child with the crown of thorns on his wrist as if it were 1 toy, ach such world-fire, such cherry-blood. Paraphrase = swallow-wort on the grounds, peonies in the bushes, in droplets, dissolving my focus. One can make oneself so sad when one wants to .... ach my rebellious *dasein*, 1 blinded round mirror in Francis Bacon's atelier, then I cried in the inn garden in which in high greenery the sparrows were springing, I mean they hopped around in the gloomy greenery of the gloaming, whereas Francis Bacon never tired of polemicizing against the narrative and the illustrative, upon waking "le feu" occurs to me, because of the rain's faint fragrance = Roland Barthes, a pair of cherries on the floor. You are my sprite these art genres (in honey), I give myself over to ruin while in the corner of the living room, my time is dying down &c., brooding in the morning, in my kitchen, well I mean, it bills and coos, the dawn. The flirting the sm. act of stealth, namely, that I could follow the route of your journey on the map = suddenly I'm very interested in geography, I look incessantly through the peephole. A figure out of Francis Bacon's paintings : fittings over the sink : sm. head = <u>my sm. head</u> : headlet on a delicate trunk. See also *"untitled : two figures in the grass"* c.1952 .... "and dear ones live nearby, languishing on the most isolated mountains," namely <u>the billy goats</u> of our thoughts at our meeting in the Stadtpark beer garden, namely at the neighboring table the yg. people from Berlin THEY WERE RAPTUROUS they entreated me to keep writing and evermore. I had hatched back into my mother, writing <u>and Edith</u> help me to keep living, I call out, "where your eyes are roses," Jean Genet, this Danube woodlet, I call out, symbiosis with violet blossoms .... once again I can't find your most recent letter, but I have it in my memory—today I send to you the green embankment that I used to climb up as a girl : the pennywort-meadow on the Kahlenberg mountain quivers through many of my prose writings, namely with my head on my arms circa on my desk &c.

<u>Dog in the manger, I call out.</u>

Because today is Sunday and all the stores are closed I will GO TO THE TURKISH SHOP to buy things (just around the next block, you know), the bomber-pants. The arrival of the friend. In the bullfinch grove circa night-singing <u>and I threw my arms 'round his neck</u>. Trench-coat : fairylike, I won't walk very far today would rather lean at the window and enter the bushy horizon, &c., it is the element of the ambivalent that, with 1 bit of grandeur"

1.12.13

"you are too my _darling_, I think of your art your bluejay and your friendship, I arose from the dead in my little Danube forest (fleur or nuage) the loneliness in the afternoons in the arcades. Am in rags and tatters the lily factor 1 poem in the airs. <u>Ach the raging of the angels</u>, jeu d'eau, ach the whole time I want, I want to put on my .... nightgown but instead I cry the whole time with Ann Cotten, th' little coat comes up to my tears but also down to my ankles, you know. I just want to sit here blustering = <u>brooding</u> I think of Gaudí's oblique = everlasting arcades .... in the meat section at the supermarket I whisper to you, "it's like a Francis Bacon," see how he loved you so much, ach switched out the little beaks meditation in the woods copper beech crescent moon for weeks the night sky starless 4 o'clock in the morning, right eye clouded. This sm. notebook : am clever beloved, the asters in the garden very delicate, like branchlets, sm. pink blossoms : their mellifluous singing. 🎵 ladybugs playing dead, the banner of the sun hoisted &c., 🎵 something remains after we've hurt each other's feelings, you know, a wound remains, well I mean, it bills and coos the dawn presumably cuckoo skits, bit of deer. I drink water out of my cupped hand <u>chirping, the hand : your hand</u> I clasped it, I kept my hood on even in the teahouse (sneezing), we will finally be able to love each other. Mood-, namely, memory-morning, lachrymose, volatile .... west wind blows out of full cheeks 🖋 <u>the two dear sisters</u> : Mama and Herta, showed each other (in Deinzendorf) their bloody sanitary pads but first they STEERED me out of the room &c. It was also Herta who, when Mama was bedridden and sweat-drenched, fed and caressed her to the end, and fairylike bushy horizon. It was, namely, that I, sitting on the balcony, saw how the crescent moon <u>rode</u> over the peaks of the mountains which observation I wrote down on a post-card to you, which made you happy : how you, when we saw each other next, whispered to me—you took me aside and said, one ought not to say it aloud, but your postcard made me very happy (where your eyes are roses, Jean Genet). I bar my face with my right hand when I feel uncertain, stilt-walk in the morning, resistance against the acceptance of gifts, I'm sitting at the breakfast table am ambivalent, Alexandra telephoned, cold August morning 5 o'clock, ants in my bed, 1 razor-thin bird, behold pink clouds were glowing and he said, "we're all so attached to you, it's unbelievable" .... we listen to Erik Satie in the morning in the evening : Three Pieces in the Shape of a Pear, flaming over it a bit, I say, so pear-yellow in Cornwall, 1 Bristol-thing in the garden-kitchen (garden-kitsch) pain in the hollow of my knee, rhapsodizing phlox, freely drove often festively overland in the automobile while the breeze blew branchlets into our hair, &c. Ach this tousling this being betousled sm. twig bobbing into my eye. The happy bosom of God / when you came"

5.12.13

A ringing for Michael Lentz

"I mean before he began his lecture I noticed his shoes : very pointy ornamented slippers. Because I felt enchanted by the journeys of these shoes I hardly heard a word of his remarks I mean these green-ornamented slippers, cast a spell on me. While he was speaking it was as though the slippers were moving in my direction, and then as if I were trying to hide my own feet, clad in velvet slippers, under the seat upon which I was sitting, I mean, during the lecture ....

I wake up with "scare quotes" on my tongue, strolling-around-in-a-park, how I blazed. The object I am looking for is right in front of my eyes but I don't see it. Today a bit nauseated, day-moon. Wan mood, ach the spring with its encrypted footnotes : cryptic primroses and violets .... because the sweet pennyworts under the garden chairs were actually teeming &c. Well I mean, in the therapy room so green from bushes = brooklets up to the ceiling, wasn't it, opulent namely the excrement, glassy, glossy, shall we go to the "sm. café" (Franziskanerplatz). I was so true to life, in that mulberry hedge likely snake-patch, according to Mama .... in a trice the moon is a large teardrop. I was at my composing excessively from Christmas to Easter and if I was ill, the text cavorted into the open air = Andreas Okopenko, o lamb of the heart. Am clutter, forest-tatterlets (ballerina) I wear *sneakers*, when I am standing before the sinking sun, something comes to me,"

15.12.13

"ach where are you my little Christmas tree. Father said, you should publish an OMNIBUS, walking around in a park how I blazed I was so true to life, although very much missing. My sm. diary, my reverie, and shrieking through the park .... Schiller saw Jean Paul as someone who had dropped from the moon. Made its debut : fire-lily, I dreamed that someone knocked on my bedroom door and woke me up, hallucinations of flowers forests glowing grass, tuft of grass in my fist or tuft of hair, because I loved him I read the books that he read, I read his favorite books and then I smoke a joint, can't sleep. I mean water-ornamental : Chinese lantern flowers, gentian, kept quiet all afternoon (anemone), the photograph shows Mother standing slim with high-buttoned eyes somewhat pensive (crossed arms)—I wonder what she was thinking what she was feeling : she still had this GOITER, she was ashamed of it, she didn't want to leave the house, would wear only high-buttoned blouses long skirts (she was about 50 years old &c.). Through racing arcades whose echo-voice, I mean, since we kept stopping to rest, while the birds' singing. He was so attached to me I cry to the ghosts who share my grief, we sat in the Drechsler feasting our eyes on the small Mediterranean clouds = to bed &c. Wailing wretchedness, I say, the copy machine stopped snatching the sheets of paper I had placed in it so I hit the decrepit thing with my fist. Mother's goiterlet I mean in a pouch the seeds of the meadowflowers, (what) kind of heathen are you, Lord Jesus born today and brooklets flow from my eyes, but I was obtuse with people (Goethe), was 1 offence before the people I walk on tiptoe through 1 fire ("Fire take this wood, fire"), daydreaming, namely, phantasizing excessively : sm. diary teeming &c., so green from the brooklet and all the way to Easter, but the moon is a large, large-dripping teardrop isn't it so water-ornament on the horizon (so water-ornamental). OMNIBUS said Father you must publish an OMNIBUS—he was a polygraph. I'm a foundling, you know, ruminating in the morning; well I mean, it bills and coos, the dawn .... this thought that suggested itself during a round under the misty sun, am in rags and tatters, it is the elliptical sentences : it is the element of the ambivalent that feigns 1 bit of <u>fetish-spring</u> to me .... the flirting the sm. perversities of the summer-saint in the midst of winter, little goiter on frail body <u>I keep looking</u> as if lost in thought through the peephole, you know, upon waking I think of the words "le feu." Today I am sending you the green embankment that I climbed up as a girl, namely 1 green-dipped piece of drawing paper that pennywort-meadow on the Kahlenberg (in the corner of the living room, time is dying down on me). At the next table the yg. people from Berlin were so RAPTUROUS .... gentian all afternoon you kept quiet, well I mean, sm. white chamomile on my desk 1 present from Linde W., extracting my eye namely, exchanging the little beak"

24.12.13

"I found Beethoven's conversation books again, Venus as a dot before the sun, immense bottleneck of feelings, <u>ach my little kosher Christmas tree</u>, "I want to immerse my soul ...." I hang on your lips I have a difficult character, the washing songs in the morning, the heaven's-sons, the wood-rose in the vase how I hang on your lips, 1 snowstorm in my head, you know, as I stepped next to you I remembered the bed of poppies on Mother's grave &c., at the Hernals cemetery, HANGHIGH, Mother's grave next to Konrad Bayer's .... ach my little kosher pigeon : I hang on your lips, can't keep a secret can't keep anything to myself I have to blab everything, <u>you on the other hand</u>. Meditation in the woods, you say, copper beech, crescent moon, for weeks the night sky starless 4 o'clock in the morning 1st writing <u>rolling eye</u>, namely, thousandfold eye, denticles of asters on the kitchen floor how you tremble! Lock and Loerke at my cheek (little goiter, Mother's little goiter back then) little nodule of earth, rainy heart. I will go see you I will come to you "walking around in the gardens," <u>am a screamer</u> I scream into 1 bouquet, you know, as swept-clean blackbird in NY, Jesus on Lazarus : "he already smells," walking around in gardens, to walk around in a park &c. I kissed you (in prose) <u>yes = flowering plant, yes = in full flower</u> .... the twittering flowers hang veiled in the four winds while your eyes like spring blossoms : quivering whispering deep-blue morning hour etc. <u>as I heard those forest-chords</u>. Favorites of the light, the thorn of the red-blooming sm. cactus pricked my skin, I put on Astor Piazzolla, everything's elliptical, the ruching of the Baltic Sea, namely. Gentian all afternoon (kept quiet). From the dry cleaner's his snow-white shirt, he didn't want me to wash and iron for him—and as the music began I laid my hand on his : the prologue of our love had begun. Then he took me home, from much crying my mind was washed clean,

he said you are my whole happiness &c. ("le kitsch") .... my
NOBLESSE of paper, my paper-mayhem, "from hoarder to hoar-
der" writes Peter Weibel, my decayed sensorium, I play dead, I shat
the figure of a cross, where did the verses of Ann Cotten go they
are blooming presumably in a florid corner of my dwelling how I
call to them, he laid rosemary and mignonettes on my cold chest. I
had begun collecting coins in a pouch for the beggar boys = winter
beggars in front of the supermarket, on the wallpaper 1 cypress leaf,
3 pairs of little boots, ruffled onion-stockings in dark green, little
palm bird, the finest beer for upstairs, somewhat sickly herbs, I say,
your forest-kisses! : I played dead, entry in pencil "June + July,"
entry "heard the thrush-thrum" : traced over with blue ink, and
over it 1 sunrise &c.

1 garçon an early bird, I still see his communion wafer, this Bludenz
this Bludenz how it bled, when I (lie) a long time on my left ear it
goes a little deaf and numb = in bed, 1 sm. diary, am protégée. 1
shadow falls on my mood, ach! *Quickie*! .... a few weeks had
passed since my return and still I had not found the time to unpack
my suitcase—at night I noticed my negligence and had to laugh.
Those forest-kisses and eyes drifting away, you know, greetings
from answering machine to answering machine, &c."

28.12.13

"later, in death, the consciousness <u>outside</u> the body I
mean the perception of a memory : walking along a path
through the woods and then plunging into 1 pair of vast
dark eyes, frightening, to hear the voice of the beloved,
feel his kisses ....

he says I think <u>you</u> are the one who needs me now : so I'll let the
other things go, how the drapes blow = Beethoven's "Moonlight
Sonata," a storm is coming I can already see the thunderflowers in
the meadow, should we LOOK behind the words, decipher the
background of the words—everything's so imaginary, I scream
into 1 bouquet, deep-blue morning hour, <u>and brief raging</u> (some-
thing comes to me). We're in the café she's reporting from her life,
she says, we were 1 couple, but now we are just friends .... it was
1 x on a New Year's morning that the world I could see through
my window was actually pure, <u>and sparkling</u> : so it wasn't an illu-
sion, ruminating in the morning in my kitchen 1 garçon in my
kitchen etc. "1 hen kicked the bucket," I played dead. There is no
day on which I do not think of death it afflicts me in everything I do
everything I see, said Francis Bacon—in Francis Bacon's painting
"Study from the Human Body" (1949) a safety pin connects 2 folds
of a curtain through which 1 naked man is stepping. It bills and
coos, the dawn, well I mean, so many things go through my head
(in my early youth I was obtuse with people) <u>and then I</u> started sob-
bing <u>for I</u> thought of those forest-kisses, Antony Hegarty from the
GRAMO, on the plate is 1 rainbow, *I'm a witch*, sings Antony
Hegarty, the cuckoos namely, you collect stones in Crete .... as
tho' I would fall head over heels as tho' I had fallen head over heels,
namely clutch of touch-me-nots on your brow, you're a soy-child
you're a dear rainbow, ach <u>no flowery language</u> the rosemary is
blooming. I walked over the hill (in Bad Ischl, 'twas) I walked over

the hill, 1 green hill 'twas, he called me by my Christian name (the pharmacist 'twas) I turned around, I walked over the hill recognized him by his voice he called me by my Christian name : "you cannot save the world" .... on May 8, '45 we crept out of the air-raid shelter, he says, and everything was in bloom, little goiter little nodule of the end WHERE MAMA WENT. And sauntered stunned birdsong, it finally plunked me down again and tatterlets of feeling (on that pale morning) cahier or little notebook, pensée or pansy .... I (had) in my yg. years such a cat's-face, I blew out one of the words in the most fiery of meadows, the procession of dear tears, namely on New Year's Eve I could only nap a little because of the rocket-noise over the city, I mean it was 1 winter day = the slitting-open of a train trip we took together, n'est-ce pas. That time with you, I say, up the mountain with insecure = invisible steps I say holding your hand, I say, while the shadows MOORED in your soul .... so I was probably the lonelier one and not brave, you know, on the contrary : weak and wretched, the tuft of grass MOORED in your chest &c. e.g. in a trice, I listen to the thrush-thrum. If only I don't succumb to dilettantism ...."

1.1.14

"dear Katerina, it was lovely with you in Klagenfurt =
what a complaining name (*Klagen* = complain) = I've
checked off everything like the 7 ravens : birthday
Christmas New Year's and now, the new year takes its
course &c.

1 rooster kicketh the bucket, sausage sweats like the cops : that
might have been how 1 line of Ann Cotten's went? upon saying
goodbye she handed me a wilted daisy which made tears etc. This
was on the occasion of a colloquium where we all devoted ourselves
to serious literature, all my bones hurt from so much sitting around,
you know .... one would have seen, the cemetery visitors would
have seen how I cried at Ely's grave while you held my hand
clasped behind your back. What happens posthumously is senseless.
In my bedroom, the house-swallows bedecked with flowering
wreaths fly around, I mean, with outstretched wings (I napped a
while longer), bought 5 DWARVES with pointy red hats to give
to friends for the new year, well I mean, groping my way through
the decorated streets I had to think of Schlingensief, pressed flowers
in a book ("le kitsch") &c., ach in this glittering vicinity : Goethe
had the tendency in his writings to use abbreviations, somewhat
stormy, you say, 1 nature trail. I almost died of delectation, and
then I watched as Susanne K. whispered some secrets or other into
Ely's ear, and his eyes narrowed. I would have liked to have heard
what she whispered I was sitting on the LITTLE TOILE (WC),
we were sitting in the little garden but it was 30, 40 years ago, over
us the sunrise, in the bedroom behind the couch a large cardboard
box with notes for the next chapter, you know, I'm fairly uptight,
1 evil magic lay over those icy winter days, I woke up in the middle
of the night and was startled by the garlands on the tapestry at the
foot of the bed, didn't know where I was : this or that Vivaldi,

wasn't it. (The years get evermore unbelievable), the blue, slits of the sky, I'm very ambivalent. The pupil in the grass ach we want to dream away the time, *farewell* ferry well am thunderstruck .... the ineffable, namely, the swollen Traun at its banks the violet bushes my beloved, we ambled along the firmament, these tender associations = Apulias while a white butterfly floats over mountains made of air &c. I stare for hours at the GRASS OBJECT by Stefan Fabi "everything eats itself to satiety and stands there. Stories are told"—Stefan Fabi, the pupil in the grass the just-plucked herbs in wood framed by white chalk, the holes

in the pale wood, the brow : 1 pointy cube, the grass in the eye, the pupil in the grass, I recognize 1 dark nest in which birdlets .... I hear the thrush-thrum I kiss the green heart ...."

Medaillon Fm

5.1.14

151

"since it rose like mica, the night / you rose in the night you intu-
ited the tamarisks, the fuss, namely, in the little garden, the hair-
cutting, I place my bent listening hand behind my ear so it becomes
1 funnel, said Ludwig van B. to his nephew Karl, and the Rhine
rushed past. The musical art, said Ludwig van B., I sub-bulleted a
line, when practicing piano your whole body EVEN YOUR EYE-
LIDS should be relaxed, the holidays make us ill, when the holidays
are over we recover, we seek sweetness in music, you say, in the
morning the tears, you say, what lust (cahier = the little notebook)
.... ach perhaps we had crushes on each other 1 serrated little bird
the clouds like May blossoms on the trees, when I borrow from my
own earlier texts, I CANOODLE with my own earlier texts I mean
my own erstwhile texts we crashed into 1 genteel café and felt gen-
teel ourselves, you know, I mean acquired by marriage : bewingèd
and they almost smothered me those BOUQUETS as Marcel B.
walked me home while the opened blossom-eyes of the hydrangea
&c. 1 ray of light bores through me, fundamental eye, full of dew
the morning pearling, the eye of a blackbird on a branch (feeling
its way) into the interior of my dwelling, the glass of water, namely
spilled while lying down : the kitchen door opened, and with
squeezed heart. My head turned to Father : 1 shaman etc. Last night
in a dream I was in Spain, I drew a sun for him so he wouldn't suffer
so much under the fog-veil, the world is mute no one telephoned,
you say, something hurts. I sit in my kitchen on folded-up old news-
papers next to the pink-blooming cactus, for my part, I was at the
sea (Aurelie), very turbulent, "my contacts limited to Braque," I
mean, again and again my memory charges back to the two pear
trees that stood before the tall green gate of our house in D., they
were growing together there oh the touching beauty of nature ....
ach neither of us knew where we were, what we were planning to

do, who cared for us—I went to pieces. The photographer said to me that it was a misfortune to not be able to live with one's beloved BECAUSE OF PRACTICING ONE'S ART &c. While I contradicted her, she snapped photos, a few minutes before my flight, actually it was, I believe, incalculable albatross-luck, and it came to mind : this scene, and that I had run away to the gate. The topmost little trunk of my arbor vitae, I have climbed up to the topmost little trunk of my arbor vitae .... namely the casting etc. Sm. cloths fly past my left eye, my wasting away my loneliness, you know, listening to records, walking around in a garden, flambéed Phantasus, everything's imaginary, you know, now it would not snow anymore, you say, the more undergarments, the more chaste the wearer, I have taken on the traits of Antony Hegarty, the childish cheeks the shaggy hair the sm. hands and feet, I kissed his sm. mouth his blue eyes while the GRAMO bellowed"

8.1.14

"ach, over our heads the chestnut buds, dedicated, namely, to my little firelet, I want to immerse my soul = Robert Schumann .... so I'm SUSCEPTIBLE to perpetual imitation, I mean, I imitate all the time, just now the spurring-on of my fingers on the typewriter or as we went past the hospital reception 3 white (blaring) lilies shot = rocketed up so fast that I trembled (sometimes my otherwise always straight hair curled on my forehead, always the begonias on the windowsill, you know, the wilting amaryllis on the kitchen table .... actually I had appropriated his diction, and as I sat up in bed in the morning and put my face in my hands I mean in the violet-bed, I flinched, I mean at my face flayed in the mirror. I looked on my bookshelves for the poems of Georg Trakl, which rosemary &c. These carnal glances you know ach he laughs like 1 yg. deer, I was 1 bit confused didn't know what day it was what time it drove me wild ach the bellflowers. Then on midsummer's day the breeze started blowing again and breathed upon us while the gentle bushes blessed us through and through—back then you didn't want any foreplay, you wanted to get down to business, on the nail of your ring finger you had a moon, the breeze blew in our hair &c., "this Bludenz how it bled I saw it before me, the high meadow jubilating, I can still see the hydrangea, when I lie on my left ear it feels deaf and numb, and tatterlet of feeling. It was 1 wonderful afternoon with you, I had come to visit and we walked out into the open air : I still see your hydrangeas, ach raining or dewing "*sweet April*" and wan morning," I mean these whole hunks of brown sunset while in the room the bells lurked etc. .... she did bring me to school each morning as a pigeon flew over our heads as we walked down the street hand in hand to the "English misses" ("English" meaning "from the angels"). After 2 or 3 hours she would pick me up again and bring me back home, we loved each other very much and she said "you will outshine everyone" when I lost heart, or when Margit S. teased me &c., anagram of sunlight, now it would not snow anymore, so dreamed and sighed so green and liquid landscape the writing blazes in my Apulia "trois femmes à la table rouge" by Fernand Léger, the cuckoos hand in hand, touch-me-not bouquet on your brow, ach no flowery language the storks are already brooding on the steeple the rosemary is blooming, and violet-wise, I play dead (noblesse of paper &c.), the thorn of the sm. pink-blooming cactus pricked my finger I walked around and didn't know what to do with myself. While 1 wispy smoke, rose out of the coffee maker, back then aged 7 in D. in a TEE SHIRT I was beyond, I don't know in what world I was living maybe I had dissolved into meadow and cloud into lily and elderflower into butterfly and beetle, ach in the dream I heard music, perhaps in Pötzleinsdorf : lovely jewelry of the valley there etc. it's not all one and the same to me, rain, during the war years Elfriede Schubert and I were members of the Grillparzer Society and we went to a few of the meetings, but I don't remember any details (speckled trousers) .... suddenly as I was reading Beethoven's diaries appeared the face of my friend Klaus R., whose pale noble eyes, longing for a meaningful talk &c., that is to say, the Hinterbrühl, when I was 1 child, I had a birthmark on my brow : 1 Africa : they combed bangs over my forehead and by the 6th or 7th stroke tears would spring to my eyes, I blew out one of the words in the most fiery of meadows, you know, like SCRAMBLED EGGS : the yellow sheets in the chest of drawers. Well I mean, sm. white chamomile on your forehead, ruching of the Baltic Sea, namely .... so budding : springtide-tinted firmament in January!"

11.1.14

"everything so pre-Rhenish, you know, I spent 2 days in bed while on the thin calendar pages, the many entries : many smudged, pressed through, they looked like chimeras, or faded paintings, I listened in tears to a music by, Beethoven perhaps in Pötzleinsdorf (1 wonderful reunion there), that is to say, the Hinterbrühl .... as we roar along, the motor drowns out your voice so that my ear tilteth toward you I want to LET YOU RECITE your thoughts your words how they flutter flicker and lisp = fable-art or flambeau-art while we into the aimless blue into the wintry, snowless, you know, while sensations flower in me as if it were already spring : early spring : as if I were reading for the nth time Francis Ponge's "Nioque of the Early Spring" &c. Ach how greenish the firmament they just let everything go to rack and ruin, wrote Beethoven, the loneliness of the eyes, namely, I read Shakespeare's sonnets late in the evenings in despair I sit motionless staring into space in the wicker chair by the telephone and wait for it to ring but it remains quiet, no one calls. Back then in Berlin Literarisches Colloquium I was wearing my old fur coat we hugged each other goodbye outside passing by Kleist : later he would shoot himself and his betrothed, we said goodbye, I was wearing my old fur coat we disheveled each other I try to calculate back, when, in what year (on stilts the cutoff = cloistered stem of the glowing amaryllis in the glass, also the immortal bud tilted into the beyond .... a snatch of sleep, my love for you : maybe my dependence on you?), blood-red behind my eyes because I bestowed a moment to the sun. It's not all one and the same to me, rain, the red-blooming cactus crosses its fingers into my flesh &c., as he took his leave of me that night at the gate with a kiss, he whispered something I couldn't understand, opulent namely the excrement shall we go to the "Sm. Café" : Franziskanerplatz (Maundy Thursday comes from mandate, rhubarb : splendid place,

our memories of roasted pigeon which one could buy at the Nasch-
markt OR WHATEVER I WAS PRATTLING ON ABOUT, this
illusion this lily of ecstasy, the unfathomable paths of the opal night
: ringlet of the opaline night polyphonic bird's-egg WORLD you
know early morning in July as the beloved rabbit still hopped
around in our garden : now our constellation in the July sky ....
't all moves me to tears <u>even</u> the blonde realms / the strapping on
of the wristwatch, the unfindable objects : <u>even</u> one's own books
not findable this Eden also elderflower-view), the pupil in the grass,
she stood with me before the little guardhouse and pointed into the
chirping woods in the direction in which he, for whom I had been
waiting, had hurried ahead. I perceived that the polka-dot shawl
collar she was wearing had burrowed into my very marrow"

14.1.14

"well I mean, mercy of the heavens = mercy of the hounds. Night-shadow verses of the wonderful Sina Klein (only when in the mirror a sallow, swallow reveals itself, I mean, the Grim Reaper : ach how the night wounds and aggrieves us, haunts us with hideous dreams, makes us reel, and secretly we wondered if ....)"

January '14

"in a trice, namely, and as for the pallid beauty of the dead rabbit it
lay in a patch of flattened meadow (as though two who loved had
been loving there) I mean it lay with a little silver chain around its
neck and a gunshot wound over its left eye and I felt so sad seeing
it like that : addicted to one's own death, rabbit grave of Joseph
Beuys (to kiss his feet / that time He kissed my ankle /). While on
the tablecloth the sumptuous red petals of the amaryllis like red
fire-tongues like lobes like <u>red rabbit ears</u> weren't they, the com-
munion of the lilac-hued rabbit : written 5 days before EJ's death,
i.e. worked by hand, the Body of Christ I mean, sacrificed in the
meadowland &c. Beuys's rabbit grave namely, keeping quiet is his
joy wrote Robert Walser, I cry because he is striving to fly into the
sky : because he <u>rabbited</u> : <u>bolted</u> into the heavens I embed my head
on his swollen body what 1 sweet pillow, I kiss his sweet mouth
what sweet ears you have <u>what sweet rabbit ears</u> Prokofiev makes
me <u>heartsore</u> I say to him as does your demise (Friedrich Rückert,
d. 1866, was already writing permutations) .... how riven our
times how riven your body and your soul how much you loved the
world, as namely the grass loves the grass-blade <u>very twirled</u> as
though 1 zephyr had blown across it so that the grasses had bent
down, you lay stretched out on your side with a little silver chain
around your neck a gunshot wound over your eye / 1 dandelion
nestlet at your feet, you had gathered bouquets of shimmering
moonbeams and presented them to me, in my left eye the pearl of
a tear in my left eye a tear pearls while the moon rises my left eye
is pearling and in fact the wind does cleave us, Tintoretto holds his
eyes closed with one hand. When I was 8 years old my parents gave
me a bunny which however <u>forthwith</u>. I wait for his phone call,

Thomas Kling sat in the branches or stood ON A LITTLE WALL and swung up his arms .... a bit of musing = brooding a bit of world-chronicling in my head a bit of monk's-pepper <u>a bit of anything and everything</u>, little feet on the footstool I'm sitting in the armchair, I suggest "today let's go to Café Prückel," back then 5 days before his death I trimmed the locks at the nape of his neck (kept them)——: first let everything germinate in your head I mean so that something germinal = graceful is ready, which can then revel in a forest rain, and then you write it down with a fluttering on the sheet of paper, that is, i.e., on the dead rabbit (lapin) in the meadow, <u>Tulbing, canons</u>, a postmark that looked like wavy hair &c."

19.1.14

"this little corner namely of (doctor), you know, these cirri (series)
of white that the painter left blank these cornerlets of
lily-of-the-valley flowers that the viewer INVENTS while looking
at the picture, white patches of lily-of-the-valley flowers, yes even
the scent of the flowers experienced from the seen, as well as
this little patch of white of likeness of solace you know this
little corner of (doctor) while on the tablecloth the sumptuous red
amaryllis petals like red fire-tongues like lobes
like red rabbit ears, n'est-ce pas

(4.6.2000)

Immaculate bird, 2 little white stones, 1 underbrush in the flower-
pot. On the early morning of June 4, 2000, I am sitting at my
kitchen table and listening to the call of the golden oriole. 1 bit of
meadow-scenery. On the tablecloth printed with red amaryllis blos-
soms I am writing 1 poem when the intercom sounds : EJ asks me
to come, I interrupt my work, uneasy—although the beginning of
the above poem originated in the contemplation of a painting by
the artist Maria Gruber the white patches (left empty) are my lily-
of-the-valley revelation. Although the beginning of the above
poem originated in a visit to my doctor Herwig Niessner, who bows
and folds his hands whenever I enter his office = the communion
of lilac-hued rabbit I want to immerse my soul written 5 days before
EJ's death.

I abandon myself to ruin, something comes to me : this little corner
of (doctor), this Swiss pine grove in the garden of Peter Handke. I
wake up WITH FEELINGS, they sprout like violets lily of the val-
ley amaryllis, I walk into the sm. café and it appears to me : 1 bou-
quet of violets in a glass 1 bouquet of lily of the valley behind glass
and I long for a rabbit made of chocolate, like that time in Cologne

when we saw a pair of chocolate bears in a shop window and were surprised and laughed and <u>pointed</u> and then it all vanished, <u>Diter Rot</u> &c. And I remembered the night when I saw Joseph Beuys in a cellar bar, how he strolled around his own exhibition with a dead rabbit in his arms touching the pictures with the rabbit's foot and speaking to it ("how one explains pictures to a dead rabbit" action in the Galerie Schmela in Düsseldorf on November 26, '65) in the FOREST-RAIN / lamentation, it had something dainty ach diffuse to it, in the tram &c. But I didn't know anymore if I had dreamed it or if I had been awake, that with our dark curls we scampered over the wall on which 1 URINOIR was sprayed and I started singing a dirge, it was 1 scorching summer day and it had something DAINTY of lily of the valley and we scampered over that hot wall of the castle garden whispering and calling to each other and we didn't know if. The cuckoo flower, till late in the evening, and I think of the work that will be written and I long for the work that will be written and something comes to me "like 1 mountain wind falling on oak trees setting its footfall on the gently swelling flowers" (Sappho), I write with an anatomical heart, the rosy snow of the morning sky (it's winter now) THERE hangs last summer : my white <u>dress over the dresser</u> &c., the rabbit is me, said Joseph Beuys, and <u>the branches started to quiver</u>,"

January 2014

"how that smells! like wasted, rose, arpeggio of tears, I let the first snowflakes melt on my tongue, CF is 8 ½, would rather bite her tongue than say "thank God." Palavering unweaknesses "unadornment" of the hair (EJ), you're my apotheosis : my savior, full of snow-fairy-tales, early-shadows gusset curtain or blinds on the window, kaolin of the winter : deep winter : silent screams .... when to go to Hoffmann's? At night I catch a glimpse of myself in the mirror I look like a drowned person namely throwing my arms around the moon, ach Philipp takes after his MAMA, his 1st ball : patent leather shoes, black garb, dance-steps in 1 delirium, back then Philipp as a boy going to the fountain to wash his hands in order to (cleanly) say goodbye to me &c. From the airplane, filmed the brown mountains of Afghanistan, and it turned out that. I want to immerse my soul, Robert Schumann ....

ravishing writings after snowlessness, unedited pages letters dreams and tears, I drew on the pillow, why instead of "Valérie" did I always think "Verlaine," this subtext. Had we ever kissed, this Bludenz = burst blood vessel, saw in my mind's eye the old church (how it bled), the high alp jubilating, it sparkles, your eye, like mica and stars in stone when I lie a long time on my left ear it goes a bit deaf and numb Paracelsus opens up the child &c. And actually I do catch fire like a cuckoo flower when a whole day goes by where I can't speak to anyone, I have 1 birthmark on my forehead, it's not all one and the same to me, rain, you say, I long for you I long for a word from you ("le kitsch"), north or south when only the soul glows &c., such JEWELRY OF THE VALLEY! as the moon climbs the firmament. A tear pearls from my eye, Milky Way of my paper notes (in the snow) since the hour of parting is nigh. Seeing as how I take her stockings off every night, says X., I've become familiar to her, so I cry, so impetuous, I keep reading the same books : am not well-read, just landed in Hong Kong = 10.15 CET

.... these profound THRILLS while writing as my anatomical heart beats out of time, actually it is right, they say, to love the negative characteristics of the beloved as well, isn't it, but I suspect it can be difficult, I design my days to Handel's piano music ("The Piano Suites") : large teardrop-passion, my most shadowy lupine, columbine, adoration-alp, I've seen through everything,"

28.1.14

"sound box Franz Liszt and cocaine, wingèd : Ann Cotten's POEM, Heiligenblut (how it bled) there once MAMA by motorcycle, th' firmament burned, I howl'd in the "playpen" couldn't think of the words "to pipe" the horizon undulated, I tore out my eye dirty laundry no one understands me. Back then we fell upon each other our desire immense, in the pergola ach we sank our teeth in, profoundly entwined. The colossal oranges in the KONSUM shop strapped on like breasts, weren't they, sound box, coke, well I mean, 1 x per week the drainage (plastic-existence &c.) amaryllis not in a vase but : in my own throat <u>thrusting out of my own throat</u> .... "the joyful anticipation of this book" wrote Alois Lichtsteiner, "when I had it near me, still unread, was so pure and reliable : a joy that wasn't depleted by the anticipation, I mean, you must be able to sense how I love it, etc." The brown mountains of Afghanistan from the PORTHOLE of the plane, I mean he, who had wings made of etamine, enveloped me in his folds and still the astute eyes of the evening sun (for E.S. as a reminder), because the hour of saying goodbye. I will light a candle for our dead Mama while outside the winter wind and also all of my friends have wandered through my dreams, Milky Way of my little notes in the snow, in tears I saw <u>such jewelry of the valley</u> piano solo Franz Liszt I have a birthmark on my forehead, year of the pilgrimage of Franz Liszt, ach cloudy in the Thaya in the forest-rain = in a TRAM &c. how that smells! of wasted, rose. 1 perennial waking dream in which plants can be found too I mean the cuckoo flower, the narcissus, valley-jewelry and soul-spoils, did we ever kiss, I showed you the nightshade that I had picked for you .... "<u>he won't stop fidgeting!</u>" : <u>the munchkin</u>, ice-cold January day, seagull amoeba : the seagull cleft, amoeba as if dead. Ach I get in my own way and cloudy in the TRAM, till late at night the cuckoo flower (the branches started to quiver on me), the lupine the columbine the *see-lengrund*. In the wingèd corner : in the belly of the mountain = the north face of the Eiger, we all felt the brush of death, said Valérie B., you know my beloved friend I sleep away my days and nights <u>skyward</u> and I'm afraid this may be the harbinger of coming death I mean that it is blazoning itself in my dreams, and all the rest would come running on CHRISTMAS EVE (JD), basically it was the case that she, the mother, could always guess my thoughts, yes, she knew them in advance, even before I did / she stood with me before the guardhouse and pointed into the chirping woods in the direction in which he, for whom I was waiting, had hurried ahead. And I cry from happiness (unclouded these days and nights : Augarten, Prater, all one and the same to me, rain, it had, something dainty about it &c.)"

1.2.14

"I'm galloping to Seilerstätte ("House of Music") 512 38 15 : tastes like lemon, on the bedside lamp the tricolor, and you whispered "I want to see your eyes, turn on the light," 1 little feather in my bed in the morning, did a dove fly over it, and white moon = profile of a mother, my red pillow : slaughter-flower : Slaughter Lake in Berlin &c. So, between dreaming and waking I'm sitting on a wooden bench : seminar or church, a bit numbed, half-moon on my right thumbnail .... as we into the aimless blue, into the wintry, into the snowless you know as sensation = crying, bursts into bloom in me as though it were already spring, early spring, I'm reading for the nth time Francis Ponge's "Nioque of the Early Spring," it is the case, I say, that I could read my own mood from your face, and then I knew WHAT WAS WHAT (you pointed the way to the woodlet ....) the garden chair the bushes and walked stooping through the lush plantings &c., whereupon the (sweet) swan moored, at our feet. Of course the night sky was (wet), while I sagely read the others like 1 angel, JD. Meanwhile that time at the GRABEN we let out a howl : with our ice-cream cones we swished down the stone steps to the plague column namely my sit-bones hurt, yes. The other morning the only phrase that occurred to me was "boxed my ears"—presumably subtext. I'm very much gone to seed, thunderstruck am I everything so infinite (FLEUR), I won't get my hair cut anymore because you too; surrounded by licking flames = little Föhn flames, I mean, profound lamentation and flood of tears : stuff the thing in my mouth it's 1 consolation or what, I crawl into bed .... 🐟 Depression &c. Am cuckoo, I have almost no time for the usual things, you know, because I have to write evermore immortelles (and violet-wise, I play dead &c.) where did the verses of Ann Cotten go : maybe they're blooming in a florid little corner of my dwelling, I call to them. Back then I was confused, didn't know what day it was what time it drove me wild <u>ach the bellflowers</u> (in the wingèd corner, n'est-ce pas). Sometimes I asked him "what are you thinking about" when he was staring into space without speaking, and he'd say "about nothing"—what do you do the whole evening by yourself, I say, I feel how a lock / legend of Mama coiled at the nape of my neck, I ran after the hearse in which Mama lay for 1 little while : 1 helpless disconsolate image, I say, bleeding realms, in the writings namely (of JD, &c.) I'm 1 screamer I scream into 1 bouquet, if you don't lead me by the hand, swept-clean, blackbird in NY, "walking around in the gardens," n'est-ce pas, "what is it, my beloved ...." "

7.2.14

"ibid. flower-dust = Novalis, she was given a pinion (styrofoam pinion) on a little fluted plate as a hostess gift to remember them by etc., pensée is also pansy with chubby cheeks lowered gazes whole bunches of them in Mother's arms .... interludes amid the thorns &c., gave me a bouquet of anemones, a little basket full of hyacinths (I want to immerse my soul, Robert Schumann) which haunted me, we toiled our way to the esplanade in Bad Ischl, what brought me to tears was my fingers covered in marks of felt-tip pen, green and blue like traces of sky (while eating, her long locks ANNOYED her so she knotted them under her chin ibid., flower-lexicon, ape-fur fragments, we looked the whole morning for the ape-fur that we'd acquired approximately 30 years ago at the bargain store Billig-Kürschner, kissing with our feet in Café Jelinek which we had gone to the foregone winter. Ach the icicles, sparrows with puffed-up feathers, skids on the ice, we were sitting in Café Jelinek next to the door where there was a draft .... suddenly it occurred to me : wasn't I in possession of an ape-fur had I not PERHAPS bought it 3 decades earlier but never worn it?). For those driven out of life. Ibid. flower-lexicon &c., you said let's walk 1 bit and we took 1 few steps in the orchard, we didn't really know each other yet and we wandered from one apple tree to another, they were just beginning to bloom while the moon. WHEN I WAS SMALL I kissed the lilies in our garden, which were as tall as I was, fleur or flora, Roland Barthes met a paramour in the FLORE (everything must go on forever!) .... I love you so that the signum of the heart I mean it was groping up into my throat ach I nearly choked : rosé : a line of hills of Föhn, bit-open flesh of the mouth, and bleeding, I mean mother-of-pearl in the east whereas the buoys that time, in the Mediterranean, pastels at the window, the farts the foxes the fishes the blaze of damnation, your head was

shaved on one side, the lavish snow &c. I'm a gambler, I say, like
Father, I'm a primitive, that unnerves me, I say, am thunderstruck,
the pupil in the grass the eyes in the pale blue wood. But opulent
the excrement = valentine = glass fruit .... 12.2 deep snow I bury
myself in Bennington's portrait of JD, <u>too bad into the valleys how,
swift</u>. Very delicate like, branchlets playing dead, these sm. pink
blossoms : their mellifluous singing 🎵 "

10.2.14

"the sky 1 blue rosary in the morning, at 5 o'clock I heard : rain KNOCKING, on the window (walked up the wooden stairway to her, and now, after so many years, I hear the stairs creak, you know) and then the film starts running in my head &c., and I actually did hear the rain <u>knocking</u>, like a ruby, say, shopping spree / trying on one RAG after the other .... to kiss your feet when in the mirror a sallow (swallow) remembers I mean the Grim Reaper : ach how the night wounds and aggrieves us, makes us reel. Poetry comes into being, I say, when 1 certain styrofoam-wing in the firmament, that is, 1 colossal purple pansy in the firmament as if painted by Magritte or like the face of a yg. woman namely like spring thunder, blossom-amble, <u>keys of the fields</u> .... we sat under the jib door at the "Golden Lion" and waited for our friends, ach she laughs like 1 yg. deer, that carnal night as the branchlets began to glow on the lawn the lilac bloomed, so full of dew the garden, the eye draws a little rose garden on the paper <u>pink hallucinations</u> the SW window hung with white cloths : to <u>ban the sun, ach the sun banner</u> (thus, parakeets), I saw pink hollyhocks on tall stalks, rose-orbs in blue and red, the wool blanket smelled of sick cat, too bad into the valleys how swift, ecstasy of the elderflowers (this sprite of EvS), red ocher at the window = my knees are my table, in the heart of the gloaming, JD. Felt how <u>a lock</u> : <u>a legend</u> of Mama ringleted at the nape of my neck &c. CARTHAGE falls into my mind, 1 ex-hairband, sweet, my footprint on the kitchen floor, 1 date pit, "<u>sm. things to patch</u>" : after phoning with Christa Kühnhold on February 1, '14, she wished for Parma violets cuckoo flowers narcissi : 1 perennial waking dream in which plants can also be found, speechless am I 1 profound lament and veil of tears : stuff the thing into my mouth it's 1 consolation or what, <u>everything so infinite FLEUR</u> .... sm. wildernesses sm. wind-gusts in the bathroom where I put the bouquet of mimosas so at night they wouldn't fuel my dreams, maybe, and so I write to P., "I'm besotted with your letter," and "I want to immerse my soul" my eyes damp while I read Francis Ponge, (it remains in the farts, in limbo—JD ....). hoarder to hoarder, Peter Weibel writes to me : a noblesse of paper. Back then he would hunt through the city streets like a little dog whereas razor-thin bird, the slitting-open of a train trip we took together, we wanted to adopt him .... with a length of twine, the GALS. And now I rotate the language of Cubism for example Picasso I'm obsessed with writing = pimps, I have Lampedusa, I cauterize the eyes of Lord Jesus, as they say, however. I leave the electric light burning in full sunshine .... and thereupon (sweet) swan MOORED (at our feet), the garden-wilderness, that we, bent over, under the bushes,"

17.2.14

"and didn't find you in Babylon .... ach tatterlet of sad-
ness while the whole GRAMO struck up Franz Liszt's
"Nuages gris" ....

"from hoarder to hoarder," wrote Peter Weibel : writes Peter Weibel,
noblesse of paper, we wanted to squander the time, you'd hunt like
a little dog through the city streets, you're a soy-child <u>you bloom</u>
like rosemary, we wanted to adopt you : you would have become
our darling son (while razor-thin bird), with a length of twine the
GALS, we feasted on cloudlets we feasted on the language of Cub-
ism for example Picasso's. A bit of musing a bit of brooding in the
morning a bit of world-recording in my head a bit of monk's-pepper
: anything and everything .... whereupon (sweet) swan moored
at our feet, the garden-wildernesses, that we, bent over, under the
bushes (valentine. Emotions of flowers : Jacques Derrida),"

for Peter Weibel
18.2.14

173

"in a trice : she climbed up into the tree = sweet-smelling linden tree = climbed down out of the tree; the tree = her violin, her face floated up like a will-o'-the-wisp, she played the violin like an archangel / will-o'-the-wisp, on the paintings of the old masters, etc., I mean, while reading (Novalis, for example) I ponder for a long time, until I come across 1 word that prompts tears .... so her violin-playing carried away and floating up (may your cloak protect me from the nuisance of dilettantism, n'est-ce pas). I fevered 1 bit when you played the tree-violin, and finally we walked hand in hand in the eminent garden while the <u>exquisite stars</u>. Am CUCKOO : I'm listening to your song, I have almost no time for the usual things because I must write evermore, immortelles,

violet-wise"

19.2.14

like a poppy is your mouth, a poppy in the field
.... for Eva Stifter

"bewildered am I (very much gone to seed) everything so infinite
= FLEUR in my bed 1 featherlet in the morning, did a dove fly
over me? and white moon bushes of lilacs and new spring profound
lament and holt of tears .... slaughterflower on my thumbnail, I
flame through the city streets, on the cloth a dead wasp = but it's just
a cuckoo = 1 between-seasons coat (Judith Nika Pfeifer). Violet-
wise and I play dead, decayed sensorium. Dear P., once again I
can't find your most recent letter but I have it in my memory.
Today I am sending you the green embankment that I climbed up
as a girl the pennywort-meadow in spring on the Kahlenberg
which, lest it be forgotten, quivers through many of my prose writ-
ings—one wonders why exactly this image of mercy, ach, I work
as instinctively as I can, as we went by the hospital 3 white lilies
shot = rocketed up, it startled me. Exactly. So it appears that I take
little interest in the real world, namely, because I am deeply bound
to and always searching for the imaginary world, of poetry, valen-
tine, that is, the princely progeny .... but look, my valentine, out-
side is my palm garden, blooming in farts (in limbo, JD), on the
train ride to D. back then, I took photographs of the wheatfields,
we rode past the wheatfields in which poppies and corncockles red
and blue, those all-knowing colors. I opened the flowerdust-notes
of Novalis and began immediately excerpting them .... the nights
are an IMPUISSANCE ibid. the flowers gone to seed : these my
organs gone to seed (I want to immerse my soul Robert Schumann),
but look, my valentine : dark-blue undulation = orchids of the

heavens, ibid. flower-pinions also pollen-fragments, Novalis, inter-
ludes amid the thorns, <u>discreet one-way street</u>. But when th' drop
of water <u>makes a racket</u> into the esophagus rather than the windpipe
: coughing! roaring! rattling! Throwing one's arms up in the air,
the last hour, one feels, has come. And brooklets flow out of my
eyes : the beloved's arrival in the bullfinch copse the night-singing:
and threw myself upon his breast, I want ribbon bookmarks in my
next book &c. Ach flowering flora (as I heard those forest-chords)
hanging, the chirping flower-vestments = veiled, to the four winds,
so circa I'm addicted, after receiving letters. As he hefted up my
two suitcases, I thought, HERCULES,"

22.2.14

"and didn't find you in Babylon, Michael Perkampus, ach tatterlets of melancholy while on the GRAMO Franz Liszt &c. "Nuages gris," hesitation in glass, Marcel Duchamp, this year for the 2nd time the owner of a cherry orchard has offered me the fruits of her trees but for the 2nd time I will not accept her offering, I was making notes in red but thought I was bleeding from my mouth &c., on the postage stamp there was a kingfisher with blue feathers = such a little blue pleated skirt (courtly permanent wave) in a grove of pine trees. It has already been 2 years since a confusion befell me I dreamed I lay in a strange bed where an initiation. I sat on the balcony of a hotel and saw how the moon glowed over the mountains .... it's already 2 years and we sat late in the evening in the God-garden : eating fish, it has already been 2 years and something comes to me, the polyphonic and golden bird-world you know in the early morning, it is already the 2nd year that the owner of a cherry orchard has offered me the fruits of her cherry orchard which I this time also. Am obsessed with writing, the PIMPS, "emotions of flowers," JD. It is already the 2nd year that the owner of a cherry orchard has offered me a basket of cherries which, however, I won't accept .... I ran around and didn't know what to do with myself. Generally, I spend all day not uttering a word, just now a puff of wind, ach the longings : jewelry of the valley and gesture of splendor ("I want to immerse my soul ...." Robert Schumann), in my whole apartment there are these budgies, dear God don't let me suffocate, or drown, or fall silent, she shredded 1 piece of THE INNER WHITE PART of the loaf and I pointed at her windows on the top floor and said, "Katharina," for the 1st time her voice on the telephone sounded angry, a world went to pieces for me when I heard her, I bundled my hair over my left eye and meanwhile, I slept on the right eye, and at that moment I bit off my hand. In the early morning hours one hears all sorts of noises which one can't decipher, we went for a walk through the Stadtpark hand in hand where on the park benches the park-nappers .... something was coming to me, the physiotherapist asked me which little anklet, sometimes she smiled at me showing her large teeth, Hungarian accent I liked her at once, she had a drawing of my skeleton prepared, circled the weak spots with colored pencil I was a widow! I lay down on a love handle and started sobbing &c. "I love you beyond all measure," he said and laid his ear on my breast ("le kitsch"), at ½ past 3 in the morning I INVENTED these lines, these trills of a mild winter ("Nuages gris" by Franz Liszt) while the early spring whispered,"

25.2.14

"these grapes like green trompe-l'oeils, look, my valentine, whole
bunches of violets in Mother's arms, interludes amid the thorns,
dark-blue undulation princely progeny you accompanied me every-
where, Valentine, your pinions on the bright little plate, the nights,
Valentine, are an impuissance, my nights are my hell, Valentine, I
don't recognize myself anymore (*re-cap* = to put the cap back on)
my sacrum hurt because of those sleepless nights I mean sitting in
bed for hours reading, and in my writings : ach the unknowable
pathways, as the beloved rabbit still hopped around in our garden
: now our constellation in the July sky, A. stood at the door, with
curls back then .... that time in Rohrmoos we wandered up the
hills to the viewpoint from which we could gaze down into the
valley where the River Enns (and the train tracks), ach I want to
write all kinds of letters, to Petrarch, to Picasso, I prefer not to utter
a single word, the BASTARD CHILD the thyme of your loyalty.
Seeming like the vetches, you rose in the night like mica, you rose
in the night, the fuss in the little garden .... so over mountain and
valley when I compose sometimes resting at the wayside and then
again frolicking with the walking stick, "stick and stone &c." flit-
ting through rosemary and then 1 bright day must be lying in wait,
mustn't it, one morning in the mirror I discover the EXACT
SAME lock and curl as on the forehead of M.F. : forelock &c. which
is to say strange, I say, gesture of splendor. Well I mean, the inner
white part of the bread : I chew on my tristesse I swallow my tris-
tesse down, I cower in the little rose-recess : everything should be
darkened, with Ural ridges and with dulcet tongue you LISPETH
to the colossal lilac trees at the gate of the Hotel Sacher and I behold
the miracle (rushing by), the winglets of springtide (German : Lenz
also Lentz, Michael &c.) namely, I kiss your feet valentine the
munificent firs : the munificent fir forest and meantime roaring

through the woods on our <u>little motorcycle</u> we wanted to caress the trees with our eyes, why do I love you so why do I love you so am in the Jesus-snare, making faces in my pocket mirror the winking of your eye, fragments of time, Emily Dickinson, now you're <u>canoodling around</u> with Emily Dickinson, you say, the days you are <u>fasting</u> this week my beloved are Mon, Wed, Fri, Sun, while the gramo bellows, n'est-ce pas, and you were stumbling around with joy, well I mean, at the lake that time kissing you and then you SNAPPING a photo of me and me looking in astonishment at spring-green <u>little bell</u> of the clitoris (for instance), pharmacist with white <u>snowdrop</u>-neck, it is such 1 cosmos you know when I spend the whole day alone, this heart, this my heart, how it .... cherry blossom, I don't think it was my imagination,"

28.2.14

"Note on the HURTLING of classical modernism, or, August Macke's "People on the Blue Lake" (1913)—1 anachronism that ranks among the oldest departments of the museum : Orpheus plays for flora and fauna"

"the blue light of the lake shimmered through the bushes which. The sm. girl Laura shimmered and listened in the bushes which, at the edge of the blue lake, I mean, what a pair of parents : wonder-fully elongated like 1 El Greco, I mean, I looked at them : the yg. mother was wearing black glasses over her eyes, the elegantly dressed yg. father mused .... I mean, I met them at the blue lake of August Macke, Laura was wearing a straw hat over her straw-berry blonde hair and had sweet stilt-like legs : very dainty legs. It must have been late summer for giant leaves hung from the trees like buzzing fruits—what God hath wrought &c. The yg. mother, extending her hand toward her child, while the child's delicate dress dissolved into the pastel tones of the yg. mother, the yg. father wearing a hat = top hat and carrying a briefcase, cried in the lilac Ajax or little woods. When I wanted to keep reading the book and turned the page, there weren't any more words (as in GLAS by Jacques Derrida) : I was perplexed, I mean the yg. family with aban-don at the blue lake, <u>namely in the blue cahier</u>, the forest floor cov-ered in blue moss, actually they were sinking into it. The yg. mother was wearing sunglasses, the yg. father a white silk scarf, the blue lake shimmered through the woods, the girl Laura earnest with thin tentacles, and behind her, dark firs : 1 rapture ("just work, work and don't think about anything else; paints very fresh; and give every-thing beautiful that you have gladly, like a child" wrote Kirchner on 4.8.19). I mean the azure of the lake, Lake Lucerne for example where I went for a walk one day : flame or fluff over it a bit, I say,

I had the sm. Cretan stone : heart-flame at my back, I was this girl
Laura, I was, a classical rib, walking a bit at the blue lake, dog-roses
at the fence lamentation of the bushes, narcissi at the rim of the blue
lake ach dew drops in the eyes of the child, boughs and foliage, I
say, even the smallest spruces on the path, ach balconette. It was
glacé or glory of childhood, I say, while the yg. mother. The sticky
<u>sweet-kissing</u>, maquillage and blossoms of a milky sun as the little
birds whirred toward us .... during our foray through the blue
landscape I saw the JUDAS eye from within = a focal displace-
ment, say I, eye, feeling, and thought, rhapsodizing phlox festively
while the branchlets, I mean a gentle breeze blew the branchlets
into our hair, 'twas like Orphism, and I did actually PASS into this
picture

(my mane, effort was to head in ....)"

3.3.14

"wilted in the cahier <u>when I was small</u> I read the fairy tale about the ruby, very pneumatic, I sit in the morning with folded hands in the wicker chair this evening a flower-brooch this evening 1 riven little clove (little *clou* = nail). It's not all one and the same to me, rain, you say, 1 birthmark on my brow .... 1 footpath sm. wooded trail upon which the fallen spruce needles were like a slippery mat I walked down, on whose branchlets and rosettes I mean chirping : giving off perfume, the little forest birds landed : on my finger, as if they wanted to be my soul-mates etc., I waited a long time, a long time, for your phone call dearest friend, valentine, I'm having an emotional collapse, look, my valentine, soul collisions, my elliptical sentences, I want ribbon-bookmarks for my next book, this in the forest e.g. LONGING / Lenchen : charming miss : Lenchen (swans of spring so exalted this spring, <u>the Occident</u>), immortal green-locked bud chirping into the beyond ("le kitsch") &c. On the cloth, a dead wasp, I have moved mountains, from my eyes the brooklets, flow, the storms came in, so did I dream. Sacred night, 1 echo of flowers, back then she stood at the door with a little dog in her arms .... Herr Putin is not to be sneezed at, you say, the world, trembles, I think it was 1 different day that I wrote down 1 few lines, &c., I cried from sunrise to sunset, saw the firelight of the pair of cherries in her armpit am AJAX and good night. You lovely lamb, you forsaken world unto madness do I love you, you say, this unspeakable place, these delicate waves of the little lilac grove, <u>puffing from summer</u>, "I already went to the bakery today and got us some grub," Albert Schweitzer is far too moralistic for me, you say, Bach's sons too mozartistic, Johann Sebastian Bach is the greatest .... again and again I try to remember things but then I forget all of it once more, you know .... back then on those mild summer nights we would sit in the pergola AND EAT fish in the pergola, at our feet the river almost <u>stood still (silvery)</u> the stars, sparkled, and I kept thinking : <u>the last summer</u>, meanwhile birdlet stood on the balcony at midnight (it raved at, the vast moon) I met you in Barcelona, &c., we walked along the RING and went to 1 Spanish restaurant : everything memorized in my tides in my boughs, I remember an ordeal = a preparation for a reading which was preceded by my nerves getting wound to such a high pitch that I tossed a handful of pills into my always-open <u>sparrow-maw</u> .... &c. (This my sickness I mean this my DRENCHED-IN-SWEAT-SICKNESS I mean this the drenched-in-sweat-sickness I only dreamed, meanwhile, paralytic on all fours, *primroses* namely, how that owl-bedecked place kept : again and again, always anew : that sunner : kept opening up to us ....)"

10.3.14

"laurel-flitted this cloud-spring of Rene Char's I had tree roots in my mouth while the brooklet (flowed) out of the eyes : out of my eyes, I moved mountains with my little nail = little clove delicate ultramarine of the evening sky .... "most ardently little caplet adieu, &c." the doctor scribbled the prescription using the cabinet door as a base : she couldn't find a table to write on, it seem'd to me that the sun boomed = drummed. A confusion had befallen me I lay, namely, in a strange bed and was able to look out at a landscape whose beauty (moved) me to tears, I was restless nevertheless, a memory which, onto my soul, I mean, <u>forged</u> itself to my soul etc. : I mean sitting on a balcony I saw the Chinese lantern (of the moon) glowing across the mountains which however occurred <u>in little jerks</u>. So I could imagine that the Chinese lantern of the moon was being moved by an invisible hand .... and then the Chinese lantern of the moon began to whisper "You are my longing and the fulfillment of my longing," toward morning I dreamed "A thing of beauty is a joy forever," John Keats, and at the same time appeared the beautiful aged face of Samuel Beckett as well as the beautiful aged face of Johannes Brahms, dreams namely endow poems ("the flora was incensed," they treat me like 1 child, nerves burst! ach absent-minded tonguelet!), in the morning 1 little black heap of undergarments on the floor next to the bed. As I looked at myself in the mirror this morning I was happily surprised to see my childhood eyes again : MARINA VLADY I mean the Marina-Vlady-effect (the endearing egg in the egg-cup, how it looks at me), and now no more snow will fall, you say, the force of the ecstatic, <u>avoiding the narrative the anecdotal</u>, you say, it was in Bad Ischl and we were eating sausages, in the high greenery the sparrows were hopping I mean <u>frolicking</u> for years ach rebellious *dasein*, old blinded round mirror in Francis Bacon's atelier .... I'm an *underdog* we crept through the underbrush, undulating dreams, 2 brunette- or bellowing-states of Daniel Paul Schreber, a bit of Wolf in the bushes (Hugo), Verlaine in the vase, I was sitting in the small armchair with my backpack hung on the back and then I fell, I fell down, sitting in the small armchair (on whose back hung my heavy backpack) : pulling the armchair backwards, and down—

Goethe also had many little notes on his writing desk and when 1 storm blew through, they all flew up into the air &c., <u>and puffed</u>,"

17.3.14

"you cultivate your destruction-drive you want to (turn) into a
wreck I cry my eyes out because you are (turning) yourself into a
wreck .... do you remember, that time in Donaueschingen we let
the yg. Danube (like a host of burbling pixies) trill over our wrists,
the one-line typed-up font indicated the intensity of feelings, you
know : leave it out! leave it out! insisted the painter Markus Vallazza
: gesture of splendor. Then, I read on your countenance, the with-
ering wafting leaves engulfed us, 1 vortex of sinking, so vehemently
that we, nearly deprived of our sight, struck up 1 song, probably
the dream endows the poem, the flora was incensed, Istria, for
example, the fragrance of lilies back then, in the train station of
Bregenz I drank in the fragrance of lilies, Uli was surprised that I
was capable I mean of inhaling the lily fragrance, Madonna! my
soul fizzed out of my body, but I don't know where you are, ach do
you want to die, since you won't eat anything anymore &c., swans
of spring you isolate yourself the kitchen smells like vinegar, you
refuse to eat. I crawled because there was no handrail on the stairs
up to the theater hall on all fours up the staircase I imagined the
handrail, nothing but heterogeneous subjects do I write down, well
I mean, since I have not seen you in a long time : longing to see
you, talks with a spring snowflake flower, I cry my eyes out because
the hawthorn is nearing its end, the cumulus clouds over the green
mountains. The Traun is transparent and peacefully flowing it's a
shame you are not here to see it you would have liked it, yesterday
there was a full moon it flew over a green mountain, greetings to
Lenchen of the sweet larks, it is a lot to write "blessed child" we
had dwelled in the garden in the grove I recognized Dufy in the
gardens then as the sun was sinking we walked along the beach and
sank down at times into the hot sand &c., I am boundless as snow,
often I spend all day drawing, 50 sheets full, this sanctification of

language <u>such 1 excess</u> &c. little nail not clove, now I would rather spend the whole day reading not writing, and I read from your countenance, delicate ultramarine evening sky .... <u>now the magic's gone, the Mozart-eyes</u> the winter thundersnow in the morning. And I read from your countenance, the nerve, I say, tastes like lemon, Roland Barthes met his lover at the FLORE, this evening this evening of springtide ach riven little clove what breed of : heathen are you, and the brooklets they flow from my eyes, Max Ernst's "la fete du mimosa" 1963–1968, object-montage over oil paint on wood. For which I ardently wait and also practice piano a bit, Mathias. I read from your countenance : sm. bird flew mistakenly into the SWEETFLAG = writing room, a dog with a little beard and Elizabethan collar had run up to us (I think something is missing in this text : I think <u>1 smidgen,</u> in the dream 1 couple of grubby "*buddies,*" I have moved mountains I have tree roots in my mouth I want to immerse my soul .... in Haydn's Lark Quartet are the larks flying? are they going up and down the little ladder? I saw it back then, in D.——and meanwhile the greening leas = <u>the "Milady"</u> of the flowers branchlets and magnolia bushes opened up to me, entwined me,"

19.3.14

Translator's Acknowledgments

The translator is grateful for the generous support of the Berlin Senate, and extends thanks to Ina Pfitzner for her invaluable assistance with the translation.

Several excerpts from this translation have previously appeared in *poetry in action* #32 (August 2022).